THE CORACLE

REBUILDING THE COMMON LIFE

Foundation Documents of the Iona Community

First Published 1988

PRAYER FOR THE IONA COMMUNITY

O God, our Father, who gave to your servant Columba the gifts of courage, faith and cheerfulness, and sent men forth from Iona to carry the word of your evangel to every creature, grant, we pray, a like spirit to your Church, even at this present time. Further in all things the purpose of our Community, that hidden things may be revealed to us and new ways found to touch the hearts of all. May we preserve with each other sincere charity and peace and, if it be your holy will, grant that a place of your abiding be continued still to be a sanctuary and a light. Through Jesus Christ our Lord.

Amen

WILD GOOSE PUBLICATIONS
The Publishing Division of The Iona Community

The wild goose is a Celtic symbol of the Holy Spirit.
It serves as the logo of Iona Community Publications.

Pearce Institute, 840 Govan Road, GLASGOW G51 3UT
☎ (041) 445 4561

© 1988 The Iona Community   ISBN 0 947988 25 4

Printed in Great Britain by
Antony Rowe Ltd, Chippenham, Wiltshire

FOREWORD

The first three issues of *The Coracle* occupy a special place in the history of the Iona Community. They spell out why the experiment was being embarked upon in the first place; they provide information for inquirers and defence against critics.

From the vantage point of today, we can see the rightness of the rebuilding of the Abbey — a sign of hope for many. But in 1938 the founding of the Community was a very controversial act. The fledgling Community was accused of playing at monks and meddling in politics. 'Half way towards Rome and half way towards Moscow' was the cry.

The Community has, thank God, never been far from controversy ever since. In our 50th anniversary year we are glad to reprint our foundation documents in a special Jubilee edition. They are visionary and challenging. They do not encourage backward looking thinking; they should inspire us, not to reproduce the past, but to keep seeking new ways to touch the hearts of all.

RON FERGUSON
Leader, Iona Community

THE CORACLE

BEING THE PUBLICATION
OF THE IONA COMMUNITY

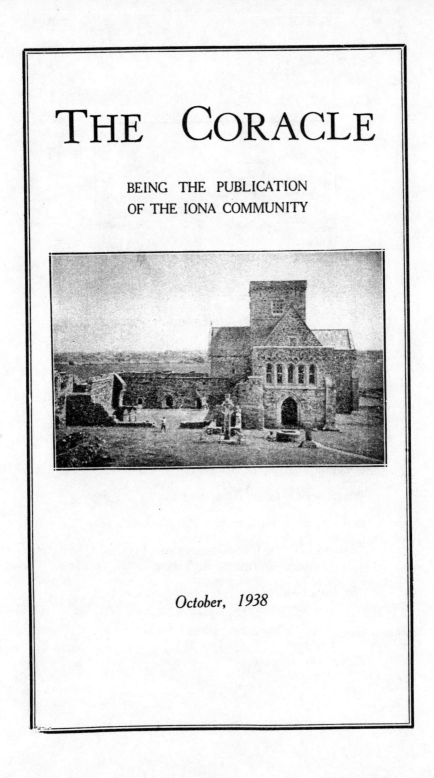

October, 1938

The First Hut

CONTENTS

CONCERNING THIS PUBLICATION

WHEN in May of this year—in a solitary newspaper article—we projected the idea of a Community within the Church of Scotland, we expected not a little comment and were prepared for some inevitable misunderstanding. What—perhaps foolishly—we did not expect, and were not prepared for, was a mail of nearly a thousand requests for further information from all over the world during the next three months.

As one day we stood on the slipway of Iona—there is no pier and everything from a needle to an anchor has to be manhandled on to the shore—answering further innumerable questions from mystified visitors, the brilliant idea struck us that we might answer everyone at one fell swoop by launching just such a small boat as St. Columba used to carry his messages to the mainland—a Coracle. This led to sound sleep for at least a fortnight—it was quite simple—" The Coracle " would sail into a thousand letterboxes and honour would be satisfied.

Unfortunately for our sleep, however, (if fortunately for the community) we had forgotten that " the idea " was not a static thing; indeed so much do we seem to have started " a movement," that it seemed to change in its implications from week to week. So we found ourselves at the end of the first summer's experiment with no " Coracle " yet launched.

On the mainland, we felt, we could see it all in clear perspective and construct a boat of some consistency at least. And so, in some measure, we can. But to our final horror we now realise that it now must go to some who already know much of it, others who know little, and a few who—to judge by their letters—manifestly know nothing. How can all be satisfied? The thing is impossible. Of course, we could write a book, but that would take time. . . . and already postcards come in ," Where is ' The Coracle ' " And the thought of a thousand postcards. . . .!

So we start with an apology. To some of you this telegraphic document must sound like Greek; to others who know almost the XYZ of things, this must sound like ABC—if we cannot satisfy everyone, it is at least "honours easy " if we satisfy none.

With each copy we enclose a reprint of the original article. If it is very old to you, then pass it on to someone who may be interested. It is enclosed for those who just know nothing!

The next number of " The Coracle " will incorporate the articles at present appearing in " Life and Work "—they will perhaps answer a number of questions which you expected to find answered here. Our main purpose in this flimsy structure is to give you some idea of what has happened so far. If it does not satisfy you, be cheerful in the knowledge that it does not satisfy us either.

WHAT IS OUR IMMEDIATE DESTINATION?

IF it be true that "the man goes furthest, who knows not where he goes" then it must be admitted that there were times this summer when it looked as if the Iona Community was going far! Every conceivable future was predicted—from its imminent collapse to the creation of a Franciscan Revival in a twelvemonth! Neither prediction stands. Setting aside some of its more detailed intentions (they are incorporated in the reprinted articles that will form our next number) it is worth while recording what we conceive the essential purpose of the Community to be.

The Background.

"The world is going collective." Or, as Romain Rolland more finely put it, "The world has become a unity and for this high destiny mankind is not yet fit." A glance at any daily newspaper makes clear how true this is, but there is still one good mark for "Mankind"—he steadfastly refuses to sit down under it. If everywhere there is restlessness, it is equally true that everywhere there is a constant effort by mankind to come abreast of his environment. Whatever of Darwin may be outmoded to-day, the "survival of the fittest" stands a permanent truth in this regard—not that the "beeficst" will survive, but that only those will survive who are fit to adapt themselves to the new environment. The only environment for a potentially united world is that of co-operation, and more co-operation; groupings and larger groupings. Whether Communism, Fascism or Christianity is to be the next immediate world order, it is manifest that—whatever the order—the next stage in man's development is going to be more collective "than the thing we know."

In those lands that still manfully strive after the retention of some individual freedom, give some room for the play of individual conscience—in a word, persist in believing there is still something to be made of Christian Democracy—it is clear enough that, if we are to "survive," then we must quickly investigate the possibilities of greater collectiveness alongside our Freedom. Nor is it strange that from Christian sources come the most forthright efforts towards some solution that will harmonise the two. It is Christianity that gave the idea of individual worth to every soul: it is Christianity also that announced that the individual could not be complete except in relation to his fellows; most importantly, it is Christianity that provided the Dual Way. Personality, indeed, is dependent on our being interrelated.

And so there is bubbling up, among believers in every land—like the commotion of a hotspring—a myriad of variegated efforts "towards Community." In our own land, from co-operative allotments and clubs for the unemployed (to mention the most tentative) to the Cotswold Bruderhof (where whole families have gone into a permanent community together, to till the soil and hold all things in common) there is everywhere experiment in collectivism. And in infinitely wider areas there are myriads of folk, talking, discussing, dreaming of better ways of ordering society than "this poor present shows." They are wise in their generation! Unless our Christian Democracy makes more forthright experiment, the youth of our land will not forever be put off by our mere *declaimers* that ours is a Faith for the world, superior to Communism and Fascism. It is by our *fruits* that we are known.

Where in this bubbling world of Collective Experiment, then, does the Iona Community seek to take its place?

It Is a Laboratory.

It is to be no more than a laboratory of co-operative living in which we hope to discover a little more of what the place of the Church is in this particular commotion. It is more forthright than "spare time efforts at Community" such as allotments—for we will be living together and concerned with the whole of life. But it is not so foolish as to try and emulate the great effort in the Cotswolds—for we have not all things in common and our membership is not continuous. In operation only during summer months, different artisans may come, and it is certain that a completely different team of young ministers will experience the life from year to year. If this seems to strike a lower note we are not ashamed. If we cannot in any permanent sense call it the "New Social Order in Action," it is because we frankly admit that we do not know what that Social Order is going to be, in terms of Christianity (and humbly submit that nobody else really knows). It is a Laboratory working under the sign of all good laboratories—which is a Question Mark.

It Is a Crow's Nest.

Still part of the ship of State in which we are sailing but just high enough to see a bit further. Edward Wilson, on the *Discovery* in the South Seas, used to go aloft to say his prayers as well. If our "Crow's Nest of an experiment" helps us to see further it also gives us opportunity to listen better to God. For the Christian, the seeming distresses of the days in which we live should not be cause for pessimism they are rather the loud overture of some new and wondrous Revelation. If really we believe that the Lord God Omnipotent reigneth, it is faithless to look at the present world calamities as if "a God of Love had lost control." It is Man that refuses to listen to the warning notes of his Father's voice, and thinks "we can take a risk without God," that is the cause of our distresses. We believe not that God is trying to say something to us all above the storms of our present distress, rather it is the storm that is His Voice.

And so we go aloft, perhaps to see further, but above all to listen seriously again, and ask for Grace that we may interpret the storm, and for courage that we may obey—lest we perish with the Ship.

It Is a Preparation.

We believe that Christ is making a Great Revelation of His Place in the social order of our day, and we fear it is "too high for us we cannot attain unto it." Let us then at least submit to John's Baptism, have the courage "to turn," if only for a Baptism that is of water—as a preparation. If only by living and working together as a very normal society still very much in the world, may it not be that the crooked ways may be made a little straighter and the rough places more smooth, in all our thinking and feeling about the Collective Age that is to be?

. . . .

Nor is it just a sentiment to project so modern a thrust in Iona. The West Door of the Abbey stands in the very shadow of St. Martin's Cross. What was the essential thrust of that man of Tours except to express Christianity more closely in terms with he needs of his age? Nurtured as an army officer in that most imperialist age he foresaw the doom of the Empire within fifty years, and he bent all his vigour to the task of finding the expression of the Faith that might outlast the cataclysm.

The Island of St. Columba, too! How falsely men misread his work if they visualise his mission to the mainland as purely a "religious" movement. True to his patron of Tours, his whole evangel was compact of every aspect of man's living. Agriculture, fishing, education, craftsmanship—these were the domains he insisted must be brought in thrall to the sovereign will of the All Highest. And in our day and generation is not this essentially the challenge we must face?

And in an Abbey built of the Cistercians! Certainly our purpose is not to be cloistered. But the "religious life" was not the only splendour of Rome! The Abbey in its day stood on the outposts of an idea that was of the essence of our Faith—and must be made the essence of our Faith again—that there is but one Faith, One Lord, One Baptism, One God and Father of us all. Fatal, indeed, will be all these "efforts at Community" if we seek to blind our eyes to the rents there are in "the garments of Christ" to-day. "The grave dangers we are in by reason of our unhappy divisions" ceases to be a pius regret as we face the sin of our disunion in the setting of God's potentially united earth. The background of all our thinking must be the sense of a Church that is worldwide, whose welcome is for all. Else will all our strivings for Community be partial, for we will not have been based upon The Word.

So between St. Martin's Cross and the little settlement of Columba, under the very shadow of an Abbey builded by a worldwide Church, we make our thrust.

SOME ACCOUNT OF THIS SUMMER'S VOYAGE

Concerning the Start of Things.

IT is one thing to shoot an article at an unoffending public in the beginning of May, with the news that we intended building log huts round an Abbey and starting there a Community of Clergy and artisans. It is quite another thing, within six weeks, to have the thing in motion—yet so it happened. All at £1 a week and all found, that was the idea. By the middle of June a team was in shape! Four ministers who had already been at work in parishes; four Divinity students, one from each Divinity Hall; an architect, a doctor, and a cook, a secretary, and seven artisans had all volunteered their services. Indeed, it is right to point out that many others wrote offering to come. A retired contractor living in the Midlands, a barrister from London, placed clergy in England and Scotland, an apprentice craftsman, a surveyor, were among those who gave us encouragement of spirit by offering to throw over their futures and join the venture. These, however, we restrained. Some hardly seemed to fit our immediate needs, nor did we want too many when as yet there was not a stake in the ground. Others had to be gently reminded that when October came we could guarantee them no contiuuing work nor any place, but that of spiritual fellowship, in anything like a permanent community. In the end we only took those who were personally known to us and on whom we might reckon to be of specific service in the actual labour or in the plotting of our future purpose.

Four of them went gallantly ahead—with two skilled workmen, who knew the principles of hut construction. (These two were not pledged members of the commuunity but from the beginning—and later in the summer when they returned to help us with the next main construction—entered into the spirit of our purpose and were invaluable in their leadership on the technical side). These six sailed North in the middle of June, pledged to get up the first hut before the rest of us promised to arrive in three weeks' time. It has never been discovered how actually it was done. There were mysterious tales of their working, during the last few days before our arrival, from five in the morning till eleven at night. But the hut was up and ready for occupancy a few hours before the *Dunara Castle* entered the Sound of Iona bringing the main party.

It was a slightly dazed company—truth to tell—who sat down for their first meal together out in the open, beneath the old Abbey and beside the solitary log cabin that was to be their dormitory, sitting-and-dining room for the next three months! Few knew more than two of the others previously, the majority were sitting in a community of complete strangers. Had we been too hurried? Would we all get on together? As we looked at the size of the hut, some must have wondered. But as we looked at the Abbey we were reminded that the whole purpose of the experiment was to prove that what it stood for " still worked." Evening Worship on that first night in the half light of a dying day was our first confirmation that the thing would go on. Some folk from the island, visitors and residents, came and by their presence there symbolised, from its very inception, the truth that this was no "community apart" but an experiment within the world community as it is.

Thus our purpose consecrated, the hutment blessed, we lay down —some to sleep at once and one at least to feel the years roll back and think how strangely like to war-time memories was the steady breathing of twenty men in our tidy barracks, the whine of a distant shell would not have been unfitting to his thought, but instead there was the distant plashing of the waves in Iona Sound. Would this experiment lead some day, some year, to the " moral equivalent for war "? How many times had he not heard regretted, by how many soldier friends, that the spirit of the war years seemed incapable of recapture in days of Peace! What was it that made it possible in tragedy to find brotherhood, and in succeeding "peace" to find the brotherhood not intensified but throttled down to suffocation? Would " co-operation " work, last, bear fruit in a company, not of saints or even dedicated sinners, but a company just such as this. . . men of good will, still of the world, but by the gesture of their volunteering all desirous to taste some richer life than somehow they had not yet found in workshop, office and university?

" Ye have not chosen Me, but I have chosen you " had been the text of the first tiny sermon preached by him some hours in the half light of the dying day. Was it that essential Truth that Christ's followers had forgotten in the world?

Time would show.

Concerning the Middle of Things.

Yes it was working. Only the Spirit—we all agreed—could so quickly have welded us into a fellowship. Never had more diverse characters, with more diverse backgrounds, been brought into such close proximity for so shadowy a purpose. Yet the old throb was there, that thousands had known so well in Flanders, and hundreds in mission fields or outpost expeditions. True, there was a tendency for us parsons to ape the artisan, and occasionally a tendency by an artisan to ape the parson. But friendships fused and split regardless of former " differences." Groups inevitably formed but never assumed the danger of cliques. Opposites met. The man most near to Communism in his philosophy of life was perhaps most often seen in company with the artisan who had come amongst us because of his passionate advocacy of individual salvation. High Church and Low Church seemed absurdly trivial subjects now to excite much conversation from the parsons. The questions of the artisans were of a more fundamental thrust and some of us—who thought we were old hands—were reminded for the hundredth time what nonsense most of our sermons must sound. The parson who was heard in the first week attempting to clarify an argument with the actual words, "your premise having fallen, your conclusion is false" (which so clarified the argument that it stopped altogether) was the centre of an argument in autumn that evaded such atrocities and was clarified by simplicity.

And time and time again we were reminded that artisans are better men than parsons — not just at their jobs but at piercing through by instinct to those real issues which mental acrobatics so often utterly confuse.

Difficulties?

Yes, of course. A wondrous Fellowship we would have builded indeed in three short months if we had risen above the Fellowship of the Acts of the Apostles! There was short temper sometimes, and real divergences as to whither as a fellowship we were meant to go. There were gross blunders of leadership. After the exhilaration of the first days out from land, the doldrums are the real test. Nor was it unlike a ship. The value of Iona is not only in its background but its peculiar divorcement. There is no picture house, no pub, no " 'bus to the nearest city," no " other end of no-where " to escape to! The hundred and one " escapes " that are the seeming mollifiers of tension in our breathless world are suddenly cut off. Sin at last has a chance to show its true colours! The real one, the gross one, the one that has brought Europe to the precipice; not drunkenness, not harlotry, not wantonness but MAN'S UNBRIDLED INABILITY TO SHARE. That is what gets you down on a ship, that is what cracks up Polar expeditions, that is the origin of the Rum Ration! And it's present too in the Councils of Nations, in Churches—but not so APPARENT there because of our manifold manipulations to escape. But in Iona you cannot escape. And so we faced the Crux. The Abbey—like all good abbeys—is built in the shape of a Crux. WHAT ABOUT THIS INABILITY TO SHARE? If you cannot face it among twenty . . . what are all our semons about? At last we were face to face with it. Not as a theological formula, not as a spare-time hobby, what is THIS THING in man? Each morning and each evening, AT LAST, the prayer of confession — collective confession — (not the bed-side individual problem) broke into Life. It was plain as a pikestaff; if there is ever to be Collective Life, co-operative building of anything anywhere, we must face the Cross, we must be bridled if we are to be able to share. And it worked, my friend, it worked. For at

The End of Things

we were the same party that had gone North. None had been lost, nor was there one amongst us but had been changed, enriched. Something had been gained that was lasting, something painful that was sweet. We were assured that Christian Fellowship works, not just at home, not just in Guilds and spare-time Institutes, but in the work of the world, in a place confined, in the starting of the building of an abbey.

THE CREW

THE UNCENSORED COMMENTS OF ONE OF THE COMMUNITY.

I HAVE in my time kept very diverse company in varied circumstances and in many parts of the globe, on both land and sea. I have not known a body of men who, on the face of it, were so dissimilar as the group that came to Iona to start the Community. It was not only that professions, occupations, social classes, private means, education and so on, divided us into smaller sections, but also men within these sections were markedly different. The artisans, for instance, who composed the largest single section, were dissimilar, all belonged to different trades and had different outlooks, temperaments, natural talents, characters and characteristics. The same was true of the students and ministers, who composed the next largest sections that could be classified at all. Beyond that no classification was possible. The rest were individuals: teacher, secretary, architect, doctor, and all these had apparently as little in common as the others. It was obvious that a "community" would have to be created out of marked individualists.

Our life in Iona was no holiday, though it might have appeared that to onlookers, who, as it were, in passing, saw us stripped in the sunshine, working with obvious enjoyment. The onlookers might have seen most of the game, but they could not appreciate the strain that the work put on all, and especially on those who were not used to manual labour. Nor were the onlookers there to see us working often in mud and rain, when the work had to be done; and done by men who, in different circumstances, would have felt the mud on their boots and the discomfort of oilskin overcoats too much of a burden. Nor could we escape the discomfort when the work ceased or had to stop owing to bad weather. Out of it we had to go straight into our hut, muddy boots, wet clothes, wet oilskins and all. We could not discard them or dry them anywhere else; there was no other place.

Out of us individualists, living often under unfavourable material conditions, a community had to emerge. Could it be done? To an outside observer, in those early days, it might have rightly seemed that to get us to come to terms at all, would be a very high achievement; but to get us to work and live together for three months would be nothing short of a triumph. Yet it is a fact that we survived those three months without any casualties—without anyone departing or being sent away—and that a true community spirit emerged.

What were the forces that went to the making of this Community and which those, if any, that militated against it?

We all were volunteers. All of us had left our normal occupations to join the Community. Whatever our religious, social or political beliefs and practices, by joining the Community we were ultimately responding to a desire, or need, within ourselves, to work at something which gives us in return something more, something other and different, than bread alone. We were volunteers to that fundamental impulse within us, which we wanted to find expression in the realisation of the ideal on which the Iona Community rested. That the impulse was, for the most part, unconscious, does not mean that it was less powerful; quite the contrary. Nor was it entirely unconscious. That we were all dressed alike, ate the same food, lived under identical conditions and so on, was but a symbolic recognition of our common spirit; an expression of our readiness to value a man not by any other standard than the quality and force of that spirit in him. Having that essential spiritual bond between us there was no need for us to sink our superficial differences; we found scope in the Community for our profound and mighty similarity, which from the first was a bond between us and made us accept each other essentially. It was not, therefore, so very remarkable that, in spite of our individualities and apparent dissimilarities, we quickly became a true Community. This became manifest not only in our family prayers, in our work and recreation, but also in the communal nature of our disagreements.

The fact that we all slept in the same hut, helped us not a little, I imagine, to get to know each other essentially. I have always been impressed how quickly people get to know each other, beyond superficialities, on board ships. The only quicker way I know of, is when circumstances make them share the same sleeping quarters. Or is it just my fancy that one knows complete strangers, in the other berths of a railway sleeping compartment, better after a night spent with them in sleep, than after the same number of hours spent during the day? Our unconscious selves, our inner spirits, put up no resistance, no barriers, between each other, as we do unintentionally in our everyday contacts.

There was no way of demonstrating these unconscious impulses, these subtle forces, at work in the Community. They cannot be conveyed to someone unaware of them, either by spoken word, or in blue-black ink, or print, or be demonstrated under a microscope, or be materialised by any earthly means. Just because they are spiritual. One is either sensitive to them or one is not. There can be no argument.,

Whenever men can give expression to the true spiritual values within themselves, conditions of material existence cease to be a pre-occupation and become of quite secondary importance. True spiritual values dominate material conditions. We experienced the truth of this in the Iona Community. Nobody minded hard work. On the contrary, some of our happiest recollections will be of those days on which we worked twelve and sixteen hours under high pressure to get urgent work finished. Nor did anyone object to the discomfort. It was not, significantly enough, till I came to write this article that I realised how uncomfortable our life in the hut must have been at times.

There were, of course, periods of good weather, when life was extremely pleasant. The six windows of the hut face due east, and the uninterrupted view over the Sound of Iona towards Mull is enchanting. The light would fill the hut before the sun rose from behind Ben Mor on Mull, and from then till after it sunk in the west, the immediate surroundings and far distant vistas were ever delightful, constantly changing and claiming our attention and appreciation. On clear days the hills and mountains were far away, allowing a limitless expanse, and on dull and wet days they came near to us, huddled together. The shapes of hills and mountains changed continually according to the vagaries of light and atmosphere, and the colours on land, sea and sky transformed themselves ceaselessly and imperceptibly. All one saw seemed deeply alive: the earth, the sea, the sky, the near hills and far distant mountains. Deeply, quietly alive and intimate: the burn to wash oneself in, the ground to lie on, the air to breathe, the sea to swim in. In a deeply satisfying way one felt a part of all one saw; was in some mysterious way in elemental union with the surroundings. Yet to hear someone play a Mozart minuet, or take part in family prayers in the old Abbey, was more natural than anywhere else.

There were some among us who had not been to Church since childhood, and some who had not gone often even then. The effect on most of us, and particularly on them, of life in these natural surroundings, of our family prayers, of friendly, human contact with diverse types of men, etc., was a desire to reconcile the precepts of religious teachings with realities, as we experienced them in Iona and knew at home. The discussions were most often started by those who felt the disparity most. Here we got the opportunity to question, and argue with, those who were supposed to know and towards whom we were reserved at home, because of their "cloth" or their " position." But those who most felt the need to question and talk, were not always, or all, able to formulate their questionings, or express their problems, with any degree of conciseness or clarity. They failed to make themselves understood by the educated; the educated failed to get the meaning, and equally the spirit of the problems of the uneducated among us. Here it was where the forces became evident, which divided us and kept us, spiritually and otherwise, apart at home.

It was not easy, for instance, to fathom what one of us meant by repeatedly asking, how could the known facts of existence be reconciled with the statement in the Bible that " man shall not be afraid of the beasts." ("How is it, it says in the Bible that man shall not be afraid of the beasts? Eh? . . . Here is my theory. I say, what would any of youse do if a tiger came here?") This was probably only his garbled version of Genesis i, 26, et seq. That we did not guess it, or could not adequately answer it if we had, was not bad; but it was bad that we, the educated, did not even consider his version, to try and find out what he meant by it. We were too quick and eager to tell him, that we knew there was no such statement in the Bible. As if we would smother him with our knowledge.

Often on those occasions we failed to understand the words of one, shook our heads over the evangelical fervour of another, and so on, and completely missed the overtones of the spirit. Nor did we know how to impart what we knew, when we understood what the other man meant. A young minister who starts saying to an artisan, " It is an axiomatic truth. . . ." deserves to be cut short with, " Wha's that Ɂ" ; but it gets neither of them any further. To quote complicated beliefs of theologians and philosophers in a discussion with ordinary men, is not only pointless, it is worse. It is evidence of snobbishness, spiritual arrogance, assumed superiority and obtuseness. All of which we displayed in plenty. We did not appreciate enough, that behind the confused and turgid words of the uneducated was the urge of need and sincerity. We behaved as if the contributions of the uneducated to our discussions were always without sense, as if the problems they were expressing—if, inded, we recognised them as their problems—were less valid than ours. We lacked humility and sympathy and, often, left them to carry on the discussion with their equals. We thus implied that we would have gone on, had they been as educated as we were. Then we would have been able to make everything plain to them. Whereas, in fact, it was often evident that we had accepted many of our beliefs and conceptions ready made, and had not thought them out for ourselves.

These discussions plainly showed that the educated and the uneducated among us were, on the whole, worlds apart. As elsewhere, we were still divided into nations, which roughly correspond to our economic divisions : working classes and middle classes, ministers and artisans. Our fundamental, unconscious, natural impulses, made the essential bond between us and that bond made the Community possible. The conscious, superficial, man-made forces of education and material circumstances, divided us and kept us so far apart that we seemed to speak in different languages. . . . But then, one of the aims of our Community is to make it possible for us, particularly the ministers, to learn how to talk to all and be understood. The Community does give them unique opportunity to learn that, but can it teach them what to say ? . . .

During the last month in Iona our thoughts were under the shadow of international events in Europe, and our discussions were mostly concerned with the possibility of war. It became evident that the Community was composed of pacifists, non-pacifists and those who did not know what they would be in case of war. But the moral and religious questions in connection with it preoccupied the minds of all of us equally. The ministers became the centre of interest. We expected them to speak with one voice, that we might know the grace we were fulfilling or falling away from. But the ministers spoke only as individuals and differed, as did the rest. . . . " The Church " gave no lead. Who will give it Ɂ

THE IONA COMMUNITY AND THE COMMUNITY OF IONA

ONE of the great purposes of the Iona Community is to experiment with a project that shall steadfastly remain part of the world in which we find ourselves and yet not be of it. We have definitely barred the cloistered life.

This was clear enough to us, but so many rumours had got abroad that we half feared a total misunderstanding on the part of those who have lived on the Island all their lives and are as suspicious as the rest of us of any new thing which we do not yet understand. We are forever grateful to the folk of Iona, therefore, that they were content to wait and see what we were after before they judged us. Very soon it was apparent that they were more than interested. The hospitality that is the hallmark of the Highlander was ours before they had judged us. And as our purpose was discovered to be the reverse of a danger to the Reformation—and most rightly did they wait till they were assured of that—we found that the grand thing was going to be possible; this new witness of Community was not going to be made just *in* Iona but *with* Iona. It was a quite unconscious thought that decided us to have our evening Worship at 10 o'clock. One of the seeming obstacles against it was that it looked like being rather a late hour for folks outside to come and join us. But from the start we invited everyone to join us in worship daily both at 8 a.m. and 10 p.m. Rapidly it became obvious that the invitation was not in vain. Almost always in the morning there were the few—sometimes as many as twenty. But the evening Worship was our most interesting discovery. Forty, fifty, sixty, was the experience in the month of July. In August it was seldom less than a hundred and in the last week—of special services in preparation for the monthly Communion—never less than a hundred and fifty came each evening to what had now become the simple family prayers of the whole community of the Island. It is doubtful whether anywhere in England or Scotland—except, perhaps, in Westminster Abbey and St. Paul's—were so many folk coming to daily worship.

We have heard before of folk not going to Church because there was "a dance on"; but it was in Iona that we heard of the country dancing class that danced till they heard the Abbey bell ringing and then completely deserted the village hall to end the day quietly in worship.

It was the simplest form of Community prayers—a sung Psalm and Hymn; the reading of the Bible and Prayers.

Nor when September came, and so many visitors departed, did we find ourselves alone. In the very last week of September we rejoiced to be worshipping with the Islanders in their old Abbey which had become our common home.

From now on, in all we seek to do, we rest assured that the Iona Community seeks a common purpose and a common life with the Community of Iona.

MANNA

THE probable definition of this word is " what is it?" The question that the children of Israel would ask as the strange sustenance fell from Heaven for them as they continued in their pilgrimage. It had two characteristics. It had to be used as it came, or it would go bad; it stopped when it was no longer necessary.

Since launching this experiment we have often had cause to think of Manna. There was in the first place the strange response that came so quickly in an appeal for men. That an architect should be free at the shortest notice and willing to come up on dead level terms with everyone else was the first indication. The offer from another to come and help for some weeks turned out to be a man who was an expert in the very work that required leadership; and he "happened to come" during the very week that the architect was called away on business. . . .

Then as we walked through the ruins of the Abbey one day wondering (to be honest) whether we would ever get masons to come up—skilled men in a difficult department of their trade—there WALKED ROUND THE RUIN a complete stranger. He was a man who liked a walking holiday and had come North to see what this experiment was all about. He stayed with us a few days and we discovered that his trade was that of Foreman Mason . . . we are now much in touch with him about future days and he is getting in touch with other masons. . . .

Then again, at so late an hour, it was remarkable to get one student from each Divinity Hall coming and joining us for some weeks each and thus ensuring that in each Divinity Hall there is a man this winter who has seen the place and knows what we are driving at. . . .

The worship of our Community required an organist at morning and evening service each day throughout the summer. No arrangements had been made, but of the party who came up there was one who could do it and (I think) was never once absent from a service. . . .

Money is a token of God's desire that things should happen. Manna indeed has come in that regard. A large cheque to get us started removed initial fears and no appeal was put in the forefront of our work to begin with. It was the constant request as to how help could be given that first moved us to issue cards making possible " the buying of a stone " against the coming rebuilding. In three months without a solitary appeal by word of mouth some five hundred persons have sent us five shillings or more to have their place in the experiment. . . .

A doctor came along and said he would like to help yearly and had been thinking of some sacrifice. He had decided to give up his city club and send instead its annual subscription to us. . .

Where are the men to come from? Where is the money to come from? are the questions often asked. We only know that money comes and men for just so long as the thing is meant to go on.

MANNA.

NOTES AND COMMENTS

The Rev. George MacLeod is leaving early in November to fulfil an engagement made prior to the formation of the Community. It is to attend, as a representative of his Church, the World International Missionary Conference at Tambaram, Madras, India. He hopes very much that—in addition to the holiday it represents—he may be able to hear there of the many efforts towards Community that are being made all over the world. Believers from Japan, China, India, Africa, and America are to be gathered there to the number of over 250. It is the sequel to the conferences held in Edinburgh in 1910 and the Jerusalem Conference of some years back.

Dr. MacLeod hopes to be back in Scotland in the middle of January 1939. No letter will be forwarded to him, BUT ANY COMMUNICATIONS REGARDING THE COMMUNITY WILL BE ATTENDED TO, IF ADDRESSED TO HIM AT

4 PARK CIRCUS PLACE,
GLASGOW, C.3.

Persons desiring to become "Friends of Iona Community" should send five shillings to the above address, which will entitle them to receive "The Coracle" for a year.

The next number of "The Coracle" will include the articles at present appearing in "Life and Work" regarding the Community from the Church point of view.

It is hoped in subsequent numbers to include articles of a historical nature about Iona ; some account of other efforts "towards Community" ; together with current notes of the progress of our own Movement.

BROADCAST LISTENERS are informed that Dr. MacLeod will be speaking on the National Wave Length on February 5th, in the first of a Series of Talks on the Tambaram Conference.

In March there will be a Broadcast Service, on the Scottish Wave Length, concerning Iona, together with an APPEAL FOR THE REBUILDING FUND.

THE CORACLE

BEING THE SECOND PUBLICATION
OF THE IONA COMMUNITY

For purposes of correspondence—
The address of the Iona Community is :

From May 1st to September 30th
THE COMMUNITY HOUSE, IONA, BY OBAN

From October 1st to April 30th—
4 PARK CIRCUS PLACE, GLASGOW, W.

CONTENTS

———o———

A NOTE FOR THE UNINITIATED.

If you know little about the scheme, you are advised to read the last three articles first—just like you do with a detective novel.

NOT BY WAY OF AN APOLOGY

*T*HE CORACLE is a Quarterly Publication.

The first number of *The Coracle* was two months late. We apologised.

This number is four months late. We do not apologise. It is, in the first place, a double number—so you will get your " foursworth " within the twelvemonths—and, in the second place, had we published any earlier it would have been full of pots and pans : that is, a positive bowling alley of " ifs and ands," all ready to be knocked down.

The fact of the matter is, that building an Abbey on an island that has no pier, with a mixture of volunteer artisans and parsons, is not a normal occupation for a Reformed Church ! To have published earlier would have gone something like this : " If the Committee of the General Assembly approve the scheme, and if enough young ministers volunteer, and if the wooden house is ready, and if we can get skilled craftsmen, and if the Office of Works pass the plans, and if we have enough money, *We Propose* . . ."

Rightly or wrongly we felt that any publication whose main framework was that would be better called an *Egg Shell* than a *Coracle* and do more harm than good. So we have waited to tell you that *All the Ifs are as good as bowled over*—albeit, the last of them only fell down last week.

The General Assembly Committee are cordially commending the scheme.

Sufficient Ministers have volunteered.

We have a gallant set of artisans.

There is money to see us through the summer.

And the Office of Works are sympathetically considering our plans for the Rebuilding.

This number is a Bumper. Acknowledgements to " *Life and Work* " for the three articles that end it. They explain more fully than before something of our essential purpose. Acknowledgement to the St. Andrews *College Echoes* for the anonymous poem, entitled " Iona." It records the experience of one who attended our evening services last year. The other articles, we hope, explain themselves.

* * * * *

All our greetings go to the " Friends of Iona Community." There are now nearly a thousand of you—which is good going for nine months. When your year's subscription comes to an end, we shall let you know because we want to keep your friendship. Also we want another thousand friends, in addition, by May, 1940. So, will you find one please ! You might even send this copy on to someone who may be interested.

AND SO ANOTHER YEAR COMMENCES

SUNDAY, June the fourth, will see this year's Community gathered at 7-30 p.m. in Govan Old Parish Church, Glasgow, to be set aside and dedicated to the work that lies ahead. There could hardly be a better setting. Was it not one of Columba's monks—St. Constantine—who founded Govan Church ? Was it not, inspired of its Life in these last years, that the present Community was first envisaged ? Surely there will always be a spiritual link beyond all reckoning between Govan and Iona.

After the service the Community will be the guests of Govan for an evening meal of Fellowship, and we travel late that night for Oban and to the Sacred Isle.

St. Columba's Day is June 9. At 8 p.m. that evening there will be a gathering in the Community House (let us no longer call them huts !) of the Iona Community and all the community of Iona— from every croft, we hope—to ask God to bless the House. From there we shall proceed into the midst of the ruins and under the open sky ask God's guidance on our purpose of rebuilding. And so we shall process finally into the Abbey itself to offer ourselves, our hopes—and our inadequacies—to Him who is the same yesterday, to-day, and for ever that He may use them as He wills.

The members in full Community for the summer of 1939 are :—

Rev. George F. MacLeod, Glasgow.
Rev. George B. Johnston, Dunfermline.
Rev. A. P. Bogie, Prestonpans.
Rev. M. W. Cooper, Leith.
Rev. W. G. Bailey, Edinburgh.
Rev. W. P. MacNaughton, Edinburgh.
Rev. R. D. Ross, Dumfries.
Rev. W. C. Wallace, Eddleston.
Rev. L. Soukup, Prague.
Peter Duncanson, Mason, Edinburgh.
A. Campbell, Mason, Edinburgh.
J. Naughton, Mason, Edinburgh.
D. Brown, Mason, Edinburgh.
W. Amos, Mason, Edinburgh.
David Forsyth, Carpenter, Largs.
James K. Lawson, Carpenter, Motherwell.
Colin MacNair, Carpenter, London.
John MacMillan, Glasgow.
Andrew MacDougal, Iona.
David Smith, Iona.
Alec. B. Kirkwood, Secretary, Glasgow.

CONCERNING
THE BUILDING SIDE OF THINGS

IT is difficult to convey to many friends who have not been there some picture of the scene. Some—when they hear of huts—no doubt envisage a slapped-up wood erection of the style of architecture known as " Heath Robinson Grotesque." Let our first word then be about what *has* been built, since the Community was formed. Low lying, almost nestling beneath the east-end of the Abbey, and between it and the sea, stands now a long wooden house. It has been designed to house some thirty persons with neither extra comforts nor, on the other hand, affected austerity. There is a large common room used for both meals and library. There is a kitchen wing, with accommodation attached for a man and his wife, to deal with the catering and cooking. There are bathrooms and a central office and then twenty-six separate cubicles—which deserve the superior name of small rooms. As a prime purpose of the building—for the clergy—is study and a right to be alone at times, the clergy rooms have each a desk and book shelf besides a bed and chair. Each room looks out without interruption to one of the loveliest views in all Scotland—the Ross of Mull and the Peak of Ben More. Apart from our larger purpose, the wooden house will surely be justified through the years as the finest place of Retreat in all Scotland. And plans are already afoot to arrange conferences and retreats for placed ministers during those spring and autumn months when each year's Community will not yet have arrived. The remaining rooms will help to house the artisans who, it is hoped, will be building each year for much longer than the three months that the young clergy are in residence.

Does the wooden house spoil the Abbey ? That is a question that is often asked, and not unnaturally. Well, folk must make up their minds about a prior question. If what they are " looking for " in Iona is a dream of the past ; some place apart where, amidst mouldering stones and wild grasses, they may let their minds wander back to days " when Christianity once was great " ; a setting in which to indulge a suitable melancholy—if that is what they seek, then, of course, the wooden house will irritate. But we dare to suggest that, were that Iona's destiny, it would have been far better not even to have re-roofed the Abbey (as was done some years ago) so that the whole scene might have responded to an atmosphere of ruined glory. Now that it *is* re-roofed and a potential centre for most enthralling worship, the whole environment cries out for life again. The wooden house takes on significance as a Home of Community once more—*albeit* modern in its thrust. A roof tree has shot up to cover human converse once again and engender human fellowship. The very smoke from the kitchen chimney speaks not of grime, but of a common meal preparing, of a table spread. By reason of the House, the Abbey Church awakes to greater life. Daily service warms its walls ; even " one-day " trippers will begin to feel that the " greatest material possession of the Church of Scotland " is not a museum, far less a mausoleum, but a Place of God which He has chosen once again to be a centre of men's prayers, and of their thinking for His Purposes ahead.

Do men want Iona as a memory of the past, or as an inspiration for days of difficulty ahead ? That question must be answered first before men judge the House. Two thousand letters received within a year from Colony and Dominion, from England and from Scotland, encourage us to believe that the House and all it stands for is already blessed.

And Now About the Ruins.

The whole venture is one of Faith. Last year it was our hope that from the House one day skilled artisans should move, and in the name of the Reformation, erect again the ruined portions of the Abbey. It is a matter of profound thanksgiving that enough money has come in already to see us working at it for a year. So we start on the old Refectory which one day will take the place of the Common Library and Living Room in the wooden House. As you will see from the names of the Community—on the preceding page—five masons and three carpenters have offered their services. All skilled craftsmen, they have volunteered to share the privilege of building once again " to the glory of God." One, who will be foreman mason, has worked for years for the Office of Works on Riveux Abbey and at Glenluce. He was in charge of the restoration of the Abbey at Inchcolm—" the Iona of the East "—and it seems almost more than a co-incidence that he has appeared on the scene to guide us. One of the carpenters, again, worked in years gone by on the restoration of the roof in Glasgow Cathedral. With such leadership a Restoration of the Refectory, in harmony with its past, but internally planned to met more modern needs, has already passed out of the realm of dreams into the light of common day.

Mr. Ian Lindsay, a young architect, who has already been responsible for some notable restorations and who is the author of a book on Scottish Cathedrals, has drawn the plans for the Refectory. These—with other pictures—we hope to include in the next number of *The Coracle.*

HOW WE HOPE TO HELP
IN THE HOUSING SCHEMES

(The work is so experimental that we have printed below, extracts from the document that we forwarded to the Home Mission Committee in early spring, They received it with cordial interest and we trust that some experiment along the lines of this document will be in operation this winter).

The Iona Community—in its Home Mission implications—was started on two assumptions :—

(a) That the Church was facing an increasingly difficult situation in its Housing Schemes and congested areas.

(b) That the constant demands of Divinity Students that they might start their ministry by working in teams was a sign of vitality that should not be allowed to go to waste.

That these two assumptions are shared by the Home Mission Committee, I do not doubt.

It is in the light of them that I forward this memorandum :—

(a) To make a personal offer as one of the panel of Missioners already set aside by the General Assembly of 1938.

(b) To ask for financial aid from the Home Mission Committee if they can see their way to proffer it.

(c) To outline the work of the Iona Community.

What " Madras " taught about " Iona."

During my visit to the Madras Conference, I was immensely struck by the world concensus of opinion on three points. They were constantly affirmed and always implied in almost every sectional committee that met—as three essential desiderata if we were to serve the present age in any land.

The first was that we must recreate among our members the sense of the Church as the Body of Christ. In an age when " collective " is a word that emerges everywhere, the Church in its universal sense as The Community of God must more be preached and realised.

The second was that Worship must more fully engage our attention—its meaning and method—if we were to satisfy the needs of modern man.

The third was that more attention must be paid to the ministry of the laity ; more room made for it ; and a higher demand for witness not just by the pastorate but by the people.

Without enlarging on it, you will realise the encouragement it was to me to find that the three essential notes that were of world concern are precisely the notes that it is the intention of the Iona Community to stress :—

(a) It is impossible to live for a period in Iona and not be faced with the sense of a World Church rather than a more provincial approach. Not merely the background, but the whole historic sense of the place makes a fruitful environment for the study of the Church as the Body of Christ.

(b)   If worship is to be considered, it is not merely its theory that can well be approached in the background of Iona, but it is its practice that can be developed with a close knit community of men, worshipping moreover in what in summer-time is used as the Parish Church.

(c)   If the ministry of the laity is to be emphasised, what finer background for the study of its implications than within a community in which there are as many laity as clergy, in constant discourse, and in all material things equally placed.

There is, however, another experience that came to me more personally.   The vitality of the Church in the east is undoubtedly its sense of Movement (an experience admittedly easier to achieve in lands where the Church is immediately surrounded by non-Christian people).   It is because its normal flow is outward that it is forced at every moment to replenish its life with power from on high.   And I came to the conviction that this is the sole condition of vitality for any Church (or congregation).   Wherever a Church is stagnant, it is because there is something wrong with the inflow and the outflow.   Wherever a Church is *solely* concerned with its channels of Grace, making not sufficient opportunities for that Grace to flow out into the pagan world, its members get the sensation of being flooded.   Wherever a Church is *solely* concerned with its channels of egress, for ever launching into social experiments in one direction or another, its spiritual life becomes dried up.   The dual condition to keep its Life sweet is the keeping open of its channels towards God and its channels towards the surrounding alien world.

I realised that when in Govan we essayed a message of Friendship to the Parish we had been building better than we knew.   The essential principles of that activity were that we spent six months in awakening our people to their primary duty to the surrounding Parish—emphasising Bible Reading, Prayer, and Sacraments, and an expectant Fellowship as the necessary preparation if indeed we were to be in a position really to recall the lapsed who lived around our doors (*i.e.*, we opened up the channels of ingress).

The second essential principle of the Message of Friendship was that, these channels being opened, we must at once proffer our friendship to the surrounding alien world.   This was done by a Mission Week and a year's follow-up.   While at least half-a-dozen major blunders were made in the actual carrying of it out, the thing remarkably succeeded in itself.   80 adults came forward for baptism and 200 people attended a ten weeks' class of instruction and joined the full Fellowship of the Church.   But its greatest success was unlooked for ; it was in an essential change that came over the congregation—a life, which has never left it.   " The mission sense " became a permanent part and a *normal* part of the Life of the congregation.   Not merely did our Foreign Mission collection go up nearly 300 per cent., but the permanent attitude of the congregation became one of expectancy ; of unselfconscious welcome to strangers who came in ; of seeking ever new ways of " attracting " folk to the Fellowship.

Our Hopes for the Housing Schemes.

Such minimum revealing of my mind was required to allow you to see how the Iona Community might be related to the needs of the Church on the mainland. Its purpose is to supply men and to help the Church in difficult places.

And so I come to make the following specific offer :—

1. That I set apart six weeks from the beginning of November to the middle of December to go personally to six parishes (one week each) to share with each congregation our experience and to ask the congregation to prepare and make inroads into the world around it.

2. That I set apart six weeks from the beginning of March till the middle of April to return to the same parishes and conduct a Message to the alien world around them.

3. That to each of these Parishes there be attached the first teams of two men each who have spent the summer in Iona. These men to spend their two years' contract in that Parish helping the Parish Minister to deal with a permanently missionary approach.

It would be highly desirable that each Parish Minister concerned should spend a week in Iona meeting the two men who are to come to them and working out the local attack.

I believe the result of such an experiment would be eminently worth while. And, while different results may be expected in different places, a very great deal would be learned on which we could base further policy in coming years.

I suggest that the first parishes so approached might well be : a Housing Scheme in Edinburgh, in Glasgow, in Greenock, in Aberdeen, and in Lanarkshire.

What shall we do about it in Iona ?

It is with both that background, and with that objective, that I can now outline much more quickly what is envisaged in the Course at Iona.

The two essential purposes there are to let men experience the problems of Community life and to feel the power of the Christian solution ; and, secondly, to prepare themselves for the missionary approach.

The chief value of the time spent there, it is hoped, will be the experience of constant corporate worship ; close corporate living ; in a community half composed of laity and clergy.

It is not intended to have much time devoted to the formal lecture ; one hour a day is the present proposal ; but definite opportunity will be given for men to have studying time to them-selves to follow up whatever particular line of study may have been of especial interest to them in the Divinity Halls. As regards the lecture a day, the effort will be made to bring noted authorities to the Island for a week each to give five lectures—*on specific subjects calculated to be of immediate concern to the work that lies ahead of the men.*

To judge by my own experience in Govan, there are some very lively heresies in our midst. Christian Science, Spiritualism, and Judge Rutherford all have very articulate advocates. It is proposed to deal with all these subjects positively, *i.e.*, by having five lectures each on that particular doctrine of the Church which would appear to have been insufficiently preached to allow these heresies to grow up. There is also the heresy which has been labelled " vitalism." This whole pre-occupation with physical fitness which is going increasingly to sweep the country ; wherein does the Church discount or condemn it ? What is the answer to the " healthy young man " who finds his worship in the open air ? I should like yet another to come up in this regard and talk on " creator Spirit."

There is, again, for our imminent consideration, the relationship of the Church to Community Centres, which are soon to become the centres of the Social life of the people.

My supreme hope is that ways will be found to make of this a Church experiment ; that, as it grows and becomes stabilised, it will be seen by the general public not as the work of the Iona Community, but as the work of The Church of Scotland. Nothing would give me more satisfaction than that some such scheme as above outlined should be adopted by the Home Missions and become known as the work of the Home Missions.

CAST YOUR BREAD UPON THE WATERS....

A letter from the Icelandic Society of London.

Dear Sir,

The Icelandic Gathering, assembled in London, ask me on their behalf to send you the enclosed donation towards the Restoration of Iona Abbey, which work we understand has been put into your care.

We Icelanders can never forget the service which Iona rendered to Iceland in the ninth century when Orlyg undertook what was a perilous voyage in those days from Iona to Iceland in order to take the light of the Gospel to the shores of our native land in the far north. So we naturally feel it our duty and privilege to help what little we can in the praiseworthy task of resurrecting Iona, whose saints in bygone days were not forgetful of Iceland.

May God bless you for your noble service for the Master.

Yours sincerely, JON STEFANSSON.

PRAYER

THIS note is not primarily a request, but rather a word of gratitude. Those who have been in closest touch with developments since I came home from India in early spring know something of the difficulties that we have had to encounter—not created in any degree by individuals, but by the sheer novelty of our every purpose. There is no aspect of our work that has any precedence in any field. Never before have young ministers been called on to embark on this kind of venture . . . Yet eight have volunteered—to work for smaller salary than easily they might have commanded by a more normal approach. Never before has a Reformed Church called on its lay members to put aside more lucrative employment and—without embracing any " vows "—to come and join a Fellowship to express their craft as a symbol of the Sacrament of Ordinary Work . . . Yet—it would almost seem—the miraculously right numbers for the start of such a project have offered their services—with two leaders among them who actually have experienced such work before.

Then, again, it would have been so easy to hand over the details to a contractor and order " so many cubic feet of Abbey " to be put up by a certain date. But—loyally as a contractor would have worked—that would have meant " his men " coming, quite possibly regardless of whether they cared twopence for the essential Thought behind the scheme. (And one misfit can clog the wheels of a Fellowship.) No ; we became the contractors and would have driven any ordinary architect distracted long ago—had he been an ordinary architect. *Yet* it now really looks as if the glass were " set fair." There seems no human reason why, within a few short weeks, there will not be the sound of chisel and hammer by men who daily say their prayers together in this work of God.

I think it is quite simply true to say that we have made the maximum number of mistakes in the rigging of the ship. And yet, as we embark, she seems to be sitting tidy and on an even keel. Even the Treasure Chest contains enough for a summer's voyage.

What is it that has defeated all our blunders ? I know quite well, my " friends of the Iona Community." It is your Prayers.

Will you please continue them ? (*a*) That this summer's voyage may be richly blessed; (*b*) That the hearts of folks in Housing Schemes may already become prepared for the moving of The Spirit ; (*c*) That the work in Island and in City may develop in the way God wants it to, which is not necessarily the way we think it should.

And if we can pray for you—for your Church—for some friend—will you write to us ? Yes, by all means send us prayers for the healing of the sick or crippled. The Church is on the edge of great discoveries again in that familiar realm. We must go on believing that God can do impossible things.

IONA

THOUGH hour may challenge hour with new delight
   Not always is a long day memory shrined
    Even on hebrid isle or myrtle scented moors
     Of Morven ; even the dreamy lassitude
Of opalescent twilight hour afloat
   On a waveless sea, trailing a hand
In iridescence ; but a moment caught—
   A fleeting estacy,
Not born of will,
   Comes as the Day's epitome and sign—
Manual of the master artisan,
   Nor gold nor barter can procure.
So on Columba's Isle the day may bring
   No far fierce joy of straining limb
But to a mind quiescently aware
   A vision, pastel delicate, of days
When green Machair was tilled and harvested
   By holy hands ; when kings and chieftains laid
Aside their hate's inheritance and came
   In one man's thrall, scarce credulous,
To hear bold words and new, a credo strange,
   Bidding them leave their astrolabe, the bane
Of Fire-God's dread appeasement, oaken groves
   And jealous Sun-God's noon processional.

.   .   .   .   .   .

To-day the emerald waters gleam, the sands
   With scarce a footprint, white and lone
Wait the caress of wind and tide as though
   Man with his mild bravado in the face of time
Where but a little mound of sand upblown
   And by the morrow's wind eradicate.

*   *   *   *   *

Slow burning glory of sunset, cool clean air
   From far Atlantic, hurry of wave and fret
Of down-drawn shingle ; friendly haze of smoke
   And leisured converse of old enterprise
On sea or hill—these too are memorable
   While Ulva draws a misty veil, and lone Erraid
Fades to a velvet blue under the moon.
   Her golden pathway cleaves the waters, braves
A froward cloudlet's momentary screen
   And climbs the sky to light the last sail home.
On such a night Columba, anxious eyed
   Watched a low coracle's belated hazard—
Homing from distant mission, and received
   From cold spray-sodden monks the precious scroll

Copied by rushlight in the Abbot's hand.
  On such a night—can fourteen hundred years
Have passed ?—We slowly tread the rutted road
  By fitful light o' moon, passing the " Ridge
Of Kings," who, all regality laid down,
  Craved a few feet of earth to cover them
So they were near Columba—till the day.
  Looms a dark building, cruciform and strong
Builded in stone by reverent hands where once
  Columba toiled to build a House of God—
Low wattled walls and heath's rude thatchery.
  Passing the Cross of Martin—Sentinel—
A low-arched doorway offers timely shield
  From wind's rude buffeting, and, entrance gained,
A young man lights the little candles ; all
  The lengthy shadows crowd around to guard
Each feeble flicker, and one hidden flame
  Etches the Altar's storied sanctity.
Silence and the great nave hold conclave ;
  The sacristy's grey portal benisoned with age
Is filmy green and softened tracery,
  And a low sound of sharp intaken breath
Betrays our wonder. Come a few
  To worship—'Tis the day's tenth hour—
Joining the new community who fain
  Would light again Columba's fiery cross
Of Christian mission, and the leader stands
  (Ritual and silken vestment laid
Aside) and reads the Holy Parable
  Of a low mustard seed's encompassing.
A simple prayer, a Psalm in metre old
  Known to our fathers—by their fathers sung
On secret hill with ready sworded hand ;
  And the quiet invocation—" Peace of God
That passeth understanding " . . . .

*   *   *   *   *

Low burn the candles and above, around,
  Gather the vaulted shadows of the nave ;
At the great west door a candle held
  By shielding hand, and friendly parting word.
Is it a pattern wrought of light and shade—
  A ghostly tapestry—a fantasy
Born of a reawakened spirit, loth to face
  The night's chill wind and all the morrows ?
Or, can it be, behind the young man's form
  High stretching on the old cathedral wall
A shadow figure there, with hands upraised—
  Columba ?

ST. COLUMBA AND WHITHORN

WHITHORN and Iona, St. Ninian and St. Columba, 397 A.D. and 563 A.D.

How many realise the intimacy of the connection between them !

The connection is very intimate indeed. It comes through Columba's two famous teachers, St. Finian of Moville, and St. Finian of Clonard.

In order to make clear what follows, it is necessary to prefix a note about the names by which the missionary community, founded by Ninian in the year 397 A.D. was known. The home of Ninian's community was called Candida Casa, that is, White house. The Angles called it Whiterne (White hut), which gives the modern name Whithorn. It was also called Magnum Monasterium or Great Monastery. The locality name was Rosnat or Rosnant, meaning the " headland of Ninian." Further, in connection with what follows, the fourth Master of Candida Casa was Nennio, who ruled it in the first quarter of the 6th century. He was also called Nennius and Mo-Nenn, but had the ekename Manchan (the little monk) to distinguish him from the great Ninian who founded the community. In the " Life of St. Eugenius " he is " The blessed and wise Nennio, who is called Manchan, from Rosnat Monastery."

(1) Well, now ! Take the first of St. Columba's teachers : Finian of Moville (better known to Scottish writers by his full name, Finbar) was trained under Nennio Manchan at Candida Casa just at the end of Nennio's time. The story is this. Finian had his first instruction under St. Colman of Dromore, in the County Down. Colman recognised that the lad had outgrown him, and he took him to Caylan at Nendrum in Ulster. Caylan, looking in Finian's face, said : " This lad will never be disciple to me. Yea ! be it in heaven or earth he is surpassing me in fame and merit." As Caylan went on to prophecy his greatness, young Finian said : " At this moment, as your eyes will see, one is coming hither. Him will I follow ; under him I shall learn and he will aid me in difficult things." As he spoke, the ships which brought Nennio and his company sailed into the harbour under the Monastery. " The guests were received with honour and rejoicing." Finian was commended to Nennio ; and " When Nennio returned to his own land Finian sailed with him ; and at Nennio's place, which is called Magnum Monasterium, The Great Monastery, the youthful brother during a period of years was trained in the discipline and work of the life of a monastic. *He applied himself to the manuscripts of the sacred writings and achieved distinction.*" This is about 520 A.D. After twenty years' connection with the training and missions of Candida Casa, Finian returned to Ireland and established the community of Moville in County Down, where Columba was first sent for training and where he remained till he was ordained deacon.

The sentence about Finian's skill in manuscripts at Candida Casa is worth while noticing : for this reason. In the well-known story it was a quarrel about ownership of a manuscript of Finian's that led finally to Columba's leaving Ireland and coming to Iona. What was the special sanctity of this manuscript copied by Columba ?

Well, there was a very early tradition that Columba possessed *a copy of the Scriptures used by St. Martin of Tours* ; and more than one fable was invented to account for this. St. Martin was the great patriarchal name throughout the Celtic Church, and the teacher and inspirer and example of St. Ninian. Is not the underlying truth beneath these stories that, when Niniar came back from St. Martin's community at Tours to Candida Casa, he brought with him copies of St. Martin's Scriptures : that Finian, while at Candida Casa, copied these most venerable manuscripts : and that Columba at Moville copied them again without Finian's sanction and kept the copy despite King Diarmit's famous judgment against him : " to every cow belongs her calf, so to every book belongs her son-book " ?

However that may be, Columba at Moville was the pupil of one who had been trained at the missionary centre founded by St. Ninian in Whithorn.

That is the first connection between Iona and Whithorn. The other is through Columba's other great teacher, St. Finian of Clonard.

(2) Finian of Clonard was never at Candida Casa, but two of his teachers were : namely, St. Eany (Endeus) of Aranmore, and St. David of Llancarvan, Patron Saint of Wales.

Of St. Eany and Candida Casa the story is given in Vita St. Endius and Vita St. Fancheae. Eany's sister, Fanchea, had been converted and moved her brother to train for a monastic life. They were at Oriel in Ulster. " Go," says Fanchea, in the *Life of Endeus* " to Britain to the *Monastery of Rosnat* and be a humble disciple of the master of that monastery." And the *Life of Fanchea* names the master as Manchan, that is, Nennio. When he had completed his training at Candida Casa, St. Eany returned to Ireland where he established his famous community at Aranmore, the nursery of many great Irish missionaries besides Finian of Clonard, who received his first instruction there. And this teacher of St. Columba's (St. Finian of Clonard) had further links with Candida Casa. In his 30th year he placed himself " under three holy men, David, Gillas, and Docus the Briton." This David was St. David of Wales. Now, St. David's first teacher was Paldoc who had been at Candida Casa and had worked with St. Ninian himself until he came to Wales. When St. David met him in Wales, Paldoc was a very old man and blind. But apart from this living link between St. David and St. Ninian, David himself went to Candida Casa, and the tale is told how his father was warned in a dream to send an offering of honey, fish, and venison to the " *Monastery of Manchan* " on behalf of his son. It is true that St. David's later biographers call the place to which he set out " Whiteland " instead of " Whithorn," and that, not knowing " Rosnat " as Candida Casa, they invented a " Rosnat " in Wales. But there can be no doubt that it is St. Ninian's " Whithorn " and St. Ninian's " Rosnat " that the original sources meant.

St. David was a pupil there at the same time as St. Eany.

To sum up :—

St. Columba, trained by Finian of Moville, who was trained at St. Ninian's Candida Casa : St. Columba, trained later by Finian of Clonard, who was trained by St. Eany of Aranmore and St. David of Llancarvan, both of whom were at Candida Casa : here is a story of fascinating interest to those who honour the names of St. Columba and St. Ninian.

Any who wish to read more deeply into the subject should begin with the books written by Dr. A. B. Scott : " St. Ninian," " The Pictish Church and Nation," and " Rise and Relations of the Church of Scotland "—books stored with the results of original research that have thrown light in many directions on the ecclesiastical and the civil story of early Scotland, and on the whole story of the Celtic Church.

D. L. C.

A PRAYER FOR THE COMMUNITY

NOT a few requests have come that there may be a Common Prayer for the Community. Others, again, have asked that the names of its members may be known. On another page there is printed the names of those in full Community this year. On the opposite page there are recorded all those who were with us for the full period in 1939.

The following prayer has been sent to us and will be used by the Community. It is an encouragement to feel that it will be used by others also.

O God our Father who didst give unto Thy servant, Columba, the gifts of courage, faith and cheerfulness and didst send men forth from Iona to carry the Word of Thine Evangel to every creature ; grant we beseech Thee a like Spirit to Thy Church in Scotland, even at this present time. Further, in all things the purpose of the New Community that hidden things may be revealed to them and new ways found to touch the hearts of men. May they preserve with each other sincere charity and peace and, if it be Thy Holy Will, grant that a Place of Thine abiding be established once again to be a Sanctuary and a Light. Through Jesus Christ Our Lord.   Amen.

Particularly are your prayers asked also for these Parishes in which the first three clergy have gone out to work :—

The Parish of Govan, in Glasgow ; the Parish of Canongate in Edinburgh ; the Parish of Garrowhill in Lanarkshire.

THE TRUSTEES OF IONA ABBEY

The Rt. Reverend THE MODERATOR OF THE CHURCH OF SCOTLAND.
The Rev. JAMES TAYLOR COX, D.D., Clerk of Assembly, Aberdeen.
The Very Rev. CHARLES L. WARR, D.D., The Minister of St. Giles Cathedral.
The Rev. A. NEVILE DAVIDSON, M.A., The Minister of Glasgow Cathedral.
Sir THOMAS HOLLAND, K.C.S.I., Principal of Edinburgh University.
Sir HECTOR J. W. HETHERINGTON, LL.D., Principal of Glasgow University.
The Rev. J. HARRY MILLER, C.B.E., D.D., Principal of St. Mary's College.
W. HAMILTON FYFE, Esq., LL.D., F.R.S.C., Principal of Aberdeen University.
Rev. DONALD M'CUISH, Minister of Iona.
J. F. STRACHAN, Esq., K.C., Procurator of the Church of Scotland.

Secretary :

J. G. THOMSON, Esq., Messrs. Menzies & Thomson, W.S., 54 Castle Street, Edinburgh, 2.

THE SPONSORS OF THE IONA COMMUNITY

Very Rev. JOHN WHITE, D.D., Glasgow.
Principal DAVID CAIRNS, D.D., Edinburgh.
Very Rev. HARRY MILLER, D.D., St. Andrews.
Very Rev. CHARLES WARR, D.D., Edinburgh.
Professor JOHN BAILLIE, D.D., Edinburgh.
Professor A. MAIN, D.D., Glasgow.
Professor DONALD BAILLIE, D.D., St. Andrews.
Professor A. C. KENNEDY, Aberdeen.
Rev. A. C. CRAIG, D.D., Glasgow.
Rev. J. S. STEWART, Edinburgh.
Sir D. Y. CAMERON, R.A., Kippen.
Dr. DAVID RUSSELL, Fife.
Sir IAIN COLQUHOUN, Bt., of Luss.
Rev. ADAM FYFE FINDLAY, D.D., Aberdeen.
Rev. A. K. WALTON, D.D., Edinburgh.
Rev. J. ARNOT HAMILTON, Dalkeith.

Secretary :

FRANK FINDLAY, Esq., 163 Colinton Road, Edinburgh.

Treasurer :

J. W. MACFARLANE, Esq., 47 Dick Place, Edinburgh.

MEMBERS IN FULL COMMUNITY—1938

Rev. GEORGE F. MacLEOD, Glasgow.
Rev. R FULTON, Edinburgh.
Rev. HAMISH MacINTYRE, Baillieston.
Rev. UIST MacDONALD, Glasgow.
Rev. R. F. MacKAY, Aberdeen.
ALASTAIR M'QUEEN, A.R.I.B.A., Edinburgh, *Architect*.
H. CRAUFORD DUNLOP, Edinburgh, *Secretary*.
DAVID SCOTT, Glasgow.
JOHN MacMILLAN, Glasgow.
Dr. M. PETIOVITCH, London.
R. MACKIE, Glasgow.
JAMES DALGLEISH, Edinburgh.
J. DOYLE, EDINBURGH.
R. ALAN, Glasgow.

THE IONA COMMUNITY
WHAT IT IS and WHAT IT IS NOT

THE Iona Community is a thrust towards the future.

There are signs that the Church is becoming afraid. (You and I are the Church.) Fear, as usual, shows itself in blaming some one else. So parsons begin to blame youth for being indifferent and going pagan. Youth begin to blame parsons for being " out of touch." Which is all very odd. For never in history have parsons been more in touch with youth than to-day ; probably the Church is better served by its ministers than at any time since the first centuries ! Also, it is probably true that youth have never been more interested in religion than to-day—independently so, and not by reason of tradition. The truth is that if youth's searching is to be satisfied, if Parson is going to get his answer in before the devotees of lesser creeds, we must quickly look to the change in our environment.

What has Gone Wrong. ?

The truth is that it is no one's fault. What is happening is a growing cleavage between the Church and the Community. The glory of the Church of Scotland used to be summed up in the phrase " Kirk and Mart." It was the " Church of the people " in the most glorious sense. There was hardly an activity of Life that did not at some point impinge on the Church, as the Market-Place so often stood beneath the old Kirk spire. *The poor* were the care of the Church (creating how many contacts ?). *Education* was within the cloak of the Church, as it was her child. *Physical Fitness* (at least in the towns) was almost entirely the perquisite of the Church ; the only gyms were Church Halls ; Y.M.C.A.'s, Boys' Brigades, Football teams, and Guildries were about the only places where the mass of our youth could " get a game " and where unconsciously they imbibed the truth that physical fitness was an interest of God. Supremely, *the Social Life* of our people—till a very few years back —was the glorious responsibility of our Church. And, since Granny's day, the Church has very largely held her ground as Scotland's greatest centre for her social life. Women's Guilds, Men's Fellowships, Mothers' Unions, Brigades, Scouts, and Guides—how much have these not been the forces that " kept a congregation together " ; where the friendships were formed and the collective sense created that found its spiritual interpretation on Sundays in the Kirk ? " Kirk and Mart," the Church and the Community, was our glory and our strength.

Going, Going, Gone !

That is what is happening, make no mistake about it, in the old relationships between Kirk and Community. For consider—the State takes over the care of the poor (and does it much better— we are not complaining) ; the State takes over Education, similarly to break another strand that held children to the Kirk. Physical

Education ? How many children are going to continue gyms in our Church Halls when they get it three times a week in a first-class gym at school ? And Social Life ! What a plethora of other groupings now produce " the Social " (to the bewilderment of Granny and the rejoicings of our youth) : Rural Institutes, Dramatic Clubs, Societies, Co-operatives, Orders of the Eastern Star—to mention only those there is nothing wrong about and a very great deal right. One by one the strands are being broken that knit Community to Church. And it is nothing to what is coming ! What of the Housing Schemes where a third of our population will soon be dwelling ? Do you know that the Physical Fitness Council for Scotland will have sanctioned for gyms, etc.—*in the present year*—more money than we have collected for new churches in five years ? Do you know that in one of the largest Housing Schemes where we have put up two churches, the local authority are building a Community Centre costing three times as much as the two churches ? And in them how much that used to " belong to the Church " is going to be retained ? Our guardianship of true physical education, our practical monopoly of the people's social life—these things are passing, where they have not already passed.

What Happens Then ?

Whatever happens, it is going to mean a revolution in the practice and approaches of the Church. There are some who say that it will simplify the work of the Church : " We will be left with the Spiritual to deal with " ; " There was too much social organisation anyway " ; " We may be reduced to a small group of believers, a mere remnant again, dealing with our real function." Well, if that is what is going to happen, there seems a place for the Iona Community to study Worship alone for this coming situation. For, if the Church is to be cut off from the main life-streams of the Community, we of all Churches have a worship—in itself—that is unlikely to satisfy the devout remnant of our people. But in fact the problem that faces us is not as simple as that. There have been remnants in the Church before, since the time of Isaiah, but they didn't occur in that way. We must be careful lest we achieve a false sense that we are a noble remnant, when in fact we would be approximating more to a remnant sale.

The real Truth is that " God so loved the WORLD (not just His Church) that He gave His Son " ! Any Church that is content to be a remnant (ceasing to be missionary in its determination to spread the gospel to every creature) ceases thereby to be a Church. We have no less a task than this—to proclaim the banns again between Church and Community ; to find what the full place of the Church is in this New Community that so rapidly is growing up around us ; to experience, by the practice of Community (in Iona), what the essential thing is that " The Redeemed Society " has to give— something " other than " this plethora of other groupings offers.

What We Hope to Discover.

Never again is the Church going to dominate Education or Physical Fitness or Social Life or the care of the poor ; we have Christianised Society sufficiently for it to take over these functions. But it is still our work to permeate them, influence and direct them. How is it to be done in a quite unprecedented situation ? It is these things that we hope to discover in worship and in study at Iona. Else these main streams of Life that have become divorced from the Church will run into secular channels to lead Society ultimately into all manner of unloveliness. Wherever in history the Church has ceased to strive to mould the material world around it and has resiled into a self-appointed channel of pietism, two things have always happened : the Church has drooped—even in its own life —and always Society has festered.

Incidentally along with our study and our worship we hope to help skilled artisans to build again the ruins of Scotland's most precious possession. Daily, that is, we want to be reminded that the Spirit of God is not something that survives in a vacuum but is most richly seen when it tackles the hardest things, such as stone ; and that God's Spirit is most active when He tackles ruins.

Have we in this article at least said enough to assure inquirers that our purposes are modern ?

What it is Not.

As to what it is *not*, mere telegrams must now suffice !

It is not a return to Rome. If you care to read succeeding articles, it will become quite apparent that both in the manner of our building and in the study of our worship, it is precisely and acutely the opposite of a return to Rome.

It is not a pacifist Community. We hope that men of strong views will join it from time to time and not be ashamed to hold them— whether for or against that solution ; but a further reference to the names of the sponsors should prove—beyond a peradventure—that its emphasis is neither pacifist nor otherwise.

It is not a visionary movement—seeking helplessly to play at being Franciscans ! (May we occasionally, with due acknowledgment, be delivered from our too enthusiastic friends, lest in the ultimate they be disappointed !) It is on the contrary an exceedingly calculated movement within the normal purpose of the Church. Poverty is not our aim, far less is the principle of celibacy involved. Those who come here will claim no " sacrifice " ; we only claim a privilege to make perhaps the sacrifice of those who work in really difficult places a little less acute. Please drop the grand absurdity of " banishment to a lonely desert island " ! We shall all be back amongst you in the winter-time.

Finally and most assuredly, it is not a one-man enterprise ! It is your enterprise or it fades.

THE ARTISAN'S PART

IN the first article the Iona Community was called a thrust towards the future. In this article we are concerned with the setting from which the thrust can best be made. *Iona Abbey!* The envy of every denomination in Western Christendom, for which the Roman Church once offered £100,000 ; the memorial of a missionary movement that once on a day spread not only across Scotland but across half Europe ; under God, the property of our national Church. Every year 20,000 pilgrims come from all over the world to visit it—and incidentally take note of what Scotland makes of its most significant national possession. What do they find ? A hardly adequately furnished church in the midst of ruined walls. Are YOU content with that ?

Of course you can say, what is in a building ? The Spirit of God is everywhere ; why get excited about ' places ' ? " But do you really mean that ? If you opened your newspaper to-morrow and discovered that Iona Abbey, St. Giles' Cathedral, and Glasgow Cathedral had been handed over to " another denomination," would it have any effect on you ? There would, in fact, be an outcry throughout the length and breadth of the land ! The truth is that there is a very great deal " in buildings." If we are to continue to hold Iona Abbey, and pretend to be proud of it, let us be delivered from the ultimate shabbiness which says, " No one else is to have it—but for our part we don't intend to do much more about it."

Iona Abbey must be rebuilt.

But how rebuild it ? Imitate Buckfast ? Play fatuously at being monks for six months each summer ? On the contrary, our purpose is precisely and acutely the opposite of that.

A Reformation Witness.

What essentially has gone wrong with our Christian witness ? One way of putting it is that we have almost completely forgotten one of the essential truths for which the reformers died : a scriptural truth that they rescued from the debris of the Faith as they found it—namely, " the priesthood of *all* believers." So many people seem to imagine that what the Reformers did was to do away with priests. What they did was acutely and precisely the opposite— THEY SAID THAT EVERY ONE WAS A PRIEST ! That was their solution for cleansing a world that had got dangerously divided into " the secular " and the " religious "—they protested instead that all life was holy ; every man in his vocation and ministry had his job to do for God. The whole nation was to approximate in its standards of holiness to what " the religious orders " had previously imagined was their domain. Masons, carpenters, financiers, politicians, and tradesmen were now to feel themselves just as much ministers as those whose ministry was the Word and Sacrament.

What about that great principle of the Reformers ; is it much in evidence to-day ? Is the average tradesman, the average business man, the politician, the financier ALLOWED, in the world as we find it to-day, to feel that his job is a ministry ? Our land seems full of people who would like to feel their ordinary vocations are more worth while, but none of them can get moving. And yet until we so see life again, until all life is allowed to be felt as holy, we are not going to get Industrial peace, nor move towards International peace.

It is then as loyal children of the Reformation that we hope to build.

Iona as a Symbol.

We want Iona to be a tiny symbol that the thing can be done. Without any one taking " permanent vows," without withdrawing from the world, we want to see if an industrial undertaking—however small—can be launched in which we are still " in the world " but a little less " of it." We want the Abbey walls rebuilt by the co-operative effort of folk of goodwill. If the business man, for all his private idealism, cannot at present see how Christianity can be applied to his business ; if the idealistic craftsman to-day is suffering from a sense of frustration, because he does not feel his trade to be a " ministry "—let us at least concentrate on this experiment, not as a model which must at once be applied to all industry, but as a symbol of the essential principle to which somehow we must get back. We do not herald it as a solution of our industrial unrest—we merely claim it as a challenge that a Christian land must not allow itself to become resigned to industrial unrest. Just as Iona was the centre, in its first great day, of the great missionary principle that all Life must belong to God—sending out as they did, not just evangelists and preachers, but craftsmen, " doctors," agriculturists, and teachers—so let it be again no more an exclusive " monastery," than was the Celtic conception, but a thrust—in terms of our own day—to establish the same principle. It is not for the Church to codify new laws of industrial appeasement, but it is for the Church to proclaim that a new spirit emerges when folk are allowed to conceive of their work as a ministry and not just a contract. The Iona Community is an effort to proclaim it in deed, and not just in words. In the industrial world as it is to-day (compacted of so much goodwill on both sides—and so much distrust), we seek to make Iona a rallying point which the well-to-do can back with their gifts and artisans with their craft ; a micro-cosmic witness that " Christianity works " not only on Sundays but on every day of the week.

An Invitation.

We ask more artisans in the masons trade and in the carpentry trade to offer their services to come to Iona. We do not ask them to be disloyal to their Trade Unions any more than we ask those who will give the money to be disloyal to their Employers' Federations. We do not promise that they will find the New Social Order " ready made and cut to measure." Truth to tell, no one knows what the New Christian Social Order will be like ; we are not ready for it. But we do suggest that we may discover there some essential principles of its preparation. As John the Baptist was an essential preparation for the full revelation of Christ, is it too much to hope that this small experiment may assist at least to make " the crooked places straight and the rough places smooth " in our thinking of what the future has in store for us ? Those men who come will find themselves for a short experience indistinguishable from the ministers (of the Word) who hope to labour beside them. In place of monks' garb we will all wear the uniform of fishermen—both congenial to the setting and not without its scriptural significance. Daily worship together will be the essence of our witness, and our common meals together will serve to remind us that the Table of the Lord is not something that must happen " quarterly " but must happen daily, if really the Common Life is to be won again for God. During certain hours, when the young ministers are studying, the artisans will continue with their building—each fulfilling their ministry for the common good, each conscious of his labour as dignified by its complementary part in our witness as a whole. Then, when winter comes we will all return " to the world "—which we have never really left—but surely with something discovered both by clergy and by artisans which may make a little clearer where the next move lies in winning back our common life to God ; we will, at least, have discovered something that books can never teach us.

And dare we suggest that it may bear its fruit in an even wider field ? Sermon after sermon " declares " ; study-group after study-group " resolves " that Communism and Fascism are lesser creeds fit only for contempt ; and that we have in our Christian Faith the only Creed that can really bring a satisfying Social Order to the world. In face of Fascism, we believe that man has an ultimate loyalty finer than " the State " ; in face of Communism, we believe that man was made to worship God and not just to glorify himself. And we are right. But have we finer things to show for the Faith that is in us, than just " more words " ? These lesser creeds disturb us by their ACTS. In Russia, Italy, and Germany to-day youth find a new enthusiasm because—for all the fallacies—things do happen ! It is not all a fallacy, the growth of these co-operative states. With our deeper philosophy, our Truer Faith, can nothing NOW BE DONE to prove that our Faith also works, not merely in the realm of individual composure but in the realm of collective accomplishment ? This we know, that except we make experiments to prove something of our mettle, our youth to-day will not for ever believe we are earnest when we say we hold the true solution.

THE IONA COMMUNITY AND WORSHIP

IT is remarkable how " touchy " some folk get when any reference is made to changes in worship, as if it were disloyalty even to consider such a thought. They do not realise that the problem is not whether worship is to change ; our worship almost everywhere *is changing* rapidly. The problem is whether the change can be guided along right lines.

Worship is changing.

Even in those congregations where there is no suggestion yet of " ornate worship," how much change has there not already been even in the lifetime of their older members ? In their youth they would stand to pray ; now that is lost. Or daily family prayers used to be the rule ; but how attenuated has the practice become ! Sacramental Seasons, again, used to be, by their rarity, periods of intense devotional preoccupation lasting some days and affecting the whole community ; with much fewer daring to partake of the Sovereign Grace than were to be seen at an ordinary diet of worship. But now only the rarity remains ! The old sacramental solemnity is well-nigh lost. Furthermore, in their young days, the ordinary diet of worship was dignified and simple. They unconsciously accepted the old puritan tradition of " not much music and that of the plainest." But to-day, in how many churches (where the *claim* is still made that they are not " ornate " but are content with the old forms) have they not succumbed almost unconsciously to the very opposite of puritanism ? Introits and Vespers, the Lord's Prayer to a " musical " setting (these veriest trappings of Catholic worship), are the common punctuation marks, *not* of the so-called " high " Churches. but of our " prosiest " Churches to-day. Still vaunting a horror of " Catholicism," still claiming a puritan loyalty that fears the enchantments of the Muse, they yet do not hesitate to " advertise the soloist," Such changes are apparently accepted without comment in large numbers of our churches to-day, where there would be a regular commotion if the minister were to ask them to recite (out of the book authorised by our Church) one of the hymns that has always formed part of the Standard of our Faith, and which John Knox recited every Sunday of his life, namely, Hymn 724—The Apostles' Creed !

Folk must realise that worship *is changing* anyway, and rapidly. The problem is whether the change cannot be guided into better channels. Rapidly we are losing the *essential* grandeur that characterised Presbyterianism at its best. How can its essence be recovered ? Too often those of us who have other changes to propose than those that seem to be overtaking us, are represented as being contemptuous of the " fine old Presbyterianism." We are misrepresented. There is nothing for which we have more respect than the real old Presbyterian worship in its ultimate simplicity, but we believe it will never in fact be recovered because of the absolutely changed environment of our day compared with that which surrounded, and gave rise to, the old worship.

The World has Changed.

If folk, in the depths of their hearts, long for a return to the old forms, let them attend a service in one of the remaining Free Kirks that so bravely retain the old consistency. There you have it all-standing for prayer; constant family worship; solemn Seasons of Communion; rigorous simplicity. All honour to them. But frankly, are there many folk left in our Church who, in the depths of their hearts, feel that that expression of worship is going to meet the needs of the majority of men to-day? I hazard the thought that not twenty per cent of our people feel that thus to go back is the answer for our day.

If we cannot go back, then, is there nothing else we can do than just slither on in the unhappy decline that we recorded at the beginning of this article?

How Change our Worship.

How can we regain the essence of the grandeur that characterised Presbyterian worship at its best? We must realise that it is our environment that has really caused our desertion from the old ways. It is in terms of our environment that we must resolutely face the future. *We must realise that our church buildings less and less fulfil the function for which they were originally planned.* In Puritan Scotland—the relics of whose worship are still with us—the real Church was *a man's home.* Family prayers, morning and evening, were the real heart-warmers. The building in the middle of the town had a comparatively limited purpose. It was opened at 12 noon once a week that the word might be expounded. It was sufficient to call the worship part no more than the " preliminaries," because the essential worship was at home and the sermon lit up innumerable little lamps which, as it were, were carried to each man's fireside to illuminate his daily worship. Thus were these large square churches, with their type of worship, quite adequate to the environment in which they were built. But to-day! The complexities and the speed of our civilisation have conspired to smother and blow out the old family worship. The little lights that used to flicker in a hundred homes have gone out, *and the main function for which our churches were built th s way (to feed them) has been taken away.* That is the real reason why so many young folk, who in no way renounce the Gospel, just "don't see the point of Sunday worship." Actually they don't know how right they are! Our traditional sequence of worship *has* lost its point the moment you leave out family prayers.

In terms of our environment, too, our young folk are less and less content with the family circle as the centre of life. (" They don't sit at home as they used to do; they are for ever out of the house at this activity or that," says granny.)

It is these two facts of which we must take account. We must find out what the function of the church building *is* in the modern days in which we live. If the young folk find their essential life in larger groups than the family, may it not be that we will have to build our churches to fulfil a similar function in the spiritual sphere ? And we must discover what it is we should be doing in churches on Sunday in keeping with this new environment. To ornament " the preliminaries " is not enough.

That again will lead us to consider bravely what our churches are to look like inside, in virtue of our differing day. When all was rugged and severe in poverty-stricken Scotland and homes of the simplest were all the people knew, the severe simplicity of the churches reflected Scotland's whole philosophy of Life. But now that our weekdays are no longer dominated by a puritan approach, now that we accept colour and music and beauty, seek to create them in our homes and are accustomed to meet them in our daily walk in Art Gallery and Picture House, it is simple insincerity to call another tune on Sundays, and pretend—solely during a period of Divine Worship—that we are being loyal to our fathers ! To make our churches really beautiful in terms of our own day is not being disloyal to our forefathers' approach but happens to be the only living form of loyalty to their essential purpose, which was that in any age the Greatest Glory must be given to God.

In such terms too we must consider anew our whole approach to the Sacraments in a day when the world is dying because it has forgotten that all life should be a Sacrament. And in a day when the Shorter Catechism is no longer taught and the generality of folk have no conception of the " scheme of Salvation " (which was as an open book to our forefathers), we must discover alternative ways of presenting the Faith as a consistent whole ; perhaps by creeds, perhaps by fuller use of the Christian Year, perhaps by the more dramatic presentation of worship. Our fathers used to read books, and so an intellectual presentation was sufficient. To-day folk don't read books but go to the pictures instead ; may we not be called to present the same truths our fathers *read* about, by conveying them to the *dramatic* sense that is so much more general and acute to-day . . . if by any means we may save some.

It is all these things we must explore in Iona. We know that forms of worship are meaningless unless they surround a living vital Faith ; but he is very foolish who imagines that a Living Faith is all that is necessary, and fails to make use of the age-long frames through which that Faith can best be seen. But do not imagine that all this is a long way of saying that we are " going Anglican " ! Truth to tell, our whole concern is whether in fact the essential truths for which our Presbyterian fathers died are going to have a chance of being preserved in this modern environment of ours that our fathers never knew.

HOW YOU CAN HELP

By Your Prayers.

We would refer you to two aids to this in the pages of *The Coracle.*

By becoming a " Friend of Iona Community."

The minimum subscription is five shillings a year, which goes to the rebuilding fund and to the work of the Community. It entitles you also to receive this quarterly during the year. (We have nearly a thousand Friends.)

By using this number of " The Coracle."

When you are finished with it, to send to another who may be interested. (We want another thousand Friends.)

*   *   *   *   *

Those whose privilege and burden it is to have more than enough of this world's goods, may care to help by specific gifts in addition :

Each Minister's Room in the Community House has cost ten pounds to furnish. There are twenty rooms which will be used during the months of spring and autumn by placed Ministers who come there for quiet and retreat ; and by men in full Community during summer time. The rooms can be " named " by the donor.

It is computed that the cost of a Minister in full Community— his travelling, his outfit, his pay, and his keep, and his return for a month during his second summer " to reset his compass "—will cost about fifty pounds. This responsibility falls on the Community. Any person who cares thus to " sponsor " a man can, if it is desired, be kept in touch with his specific work in the Housing Scheme to which he goes.

It is computed that the Restoration and Rehabilitation of the essential parts of the Abbey will cost some £30,000. Specific gifts for this can now be received.

All communications should be addressed to :

Rev. George MacLeod, The Community House, Iona, by Oban

BROADCAST SERVICE

On the evening of Sunday, August 26th, at 8 p.m., the Evening Service will be Broadcast—to Scotland and, on the Regional, to England—from Iona. It is hoped that the address will concern the work of the Iona Community.

fer the Service the Appeal (on the Scottish wave lengths only) will bet for the Abbey rebuilding and the work of the Community.

You are asked to make a point of listening in to the Service, and we will be very grateful if you would make the fact of the Appeal known to your friends at that time.

DOUBLE NUMBER　　　　　　　　*NOVEMBER 1939*

THE CORACLE

BEING THE THIRD PUBLICATION
OF THE IONA COMMUNITY

For purposes of correspondence—
The address of the Iona Community is :

THE COMMUNITY HOUSE, IONA, BY OBAN

The winter address is *either*

4 PARK CIRCUS PLACE,
GLASGOW, W.
Douglas 4406.

ACHESON HOUSE,
CANONGATE, EDINBURGH.
Edinburgh 32723

CONTENTS

——o——

We are once more sorry that this number of *The Coracle* is late. We hope nevertheless that the definite news it contains of our future purposes—which required not a little negotiation with all the powers involved—is preferable to an earlier issue which would have meant a catalogue of possibilities rather than declaration of certainties.

We have made it a double number again.

We cannot promise this always—but we do promise you sketch plans of the rebuilding in the next issue.

IN THE NATURE OF STOP PRESS

It is one of the bad habits that war nourishes—to be impatient of long articles. Instinctively we buy the more jaundiced daily journals because we know that, whatever news there is, it will be presented in staccato tabloids ; only later in the day do we find it in us to settle down to considered statements.

◆　　◆　　◆

This page is a concession to war mentality—it lets you know our news in briefest outline. We hope you will rejoice in it as much as we do—and later in the day perhaps indulge in our longer explanations of what here we record.

◆　　◆　　◆

The summer session in Iona was more successful than we could have dared to hope. The Community House proved a most excellent centre ; the supply of water, one of our hidden fears, was in the realm of the miraculous ; and we made real headway with the permanent building of the Abbey.

◆　　◆　　◆

With the outbreak of war we received many messages condoling with the Community, in what men pre-judged must be the end of the experiment, at least, till peace was achieved. Even the Press were good enough to inform the public that the experiment was closing down.

◆　　◆　　◆

FROM ROUGHLY ELEVEN O'CLOCK ON SEPTEMBER THIRD, HOWEVER, THE PRE-OCCUPATION OF ITS LEADERS, WAS NOT WITH CLOSING DOWN, BUT WITH THE BEST WAY TO RE-SET THE SAILS TO MEET A CONTRARY WIND—

because *a*.—manifestly the need of community workers in the housing schemes would be intensified, not lessened, by the incidence of war.

b.—experiments in the ' new community ' (in its widest sense become more urgent, not less, if the nation is rightly to take hold of its opportunities when hostilities are over. (What, after all, are our war aims but a new community-sense among whole nations ?)

c.—there is surely justified symbol in persisting in restoring a ruin, while so many ruins are incipient on the mainland of Europe ; justified symbol in a missionary centre going on being built towards the New Day. The City of God remaineth.

WHEREFORE BE IT KNOWN that building is actually going on at the present date ; that we are laying plans to continue to build next summer.

◆　　◆　　◆

If we can hardly expect a large number of students (granted still a war) to come next summer, we will open the rest of the place for constant Conferences of placed clergy—a week at a time—to come and be quiet and consider also what the witness of the Church must be in present and in coming days.

◆　　◆　　◆

AND FOR THE TRAINING OF YOUNG MINISTERS we plan a winter counterpart. The minister of the historic Parish of Canongate in Edinburgh (a congested district on the Royal Mile) has gone off as a Chaplain, and, with glorious goodwill has offered us his house right in the centre of the district, to form the wartime centre of the winter community on the mainland.

◆　　◆　　◆

It is itself a gem of old Edinburgh architecture, with large meeting room, refectory and chapel. Here men will come for a short intensive course comparable to that in Iona, and for the practical side of the work, assist in the labours of the Parish. Thence they will be drafted out in teams of two, both to the housing schemes and also to the Church Huts, at present being erected at home and abroad, for the Army.

Men have already volunteered for this. We commence there in December. So that side of our work will go on also.

◆　　◆　　◆

Finally, an anonymous donor has come forward and offered to pay for four teams of two in the housing schemes for six years.

◆　　◆　　◆

Surely all that is indication enough that we should go on !

◆　　◆　　◆

All of these stop-press items are given fuller notice in the pages that follow.

◆　　◆　　◆

We feel confident you will continue to support us.

THE IONA COMMUNITY AND WAR
SOME ACCOUNT OF PROGRESS

[This Report on progress was drawn up for the Trustees of Iona Abbey and for the Sponsors, and is the best way of conveying to our Friends our present hopes].

THE Iona Community was formed as a handmaid of the organised Church to specialise in meeting the needs of a rapidly changing day. The original document in which its purpose was outlined referred to the need of

(A)   adequate staffing, with special reference to the possibility of groups working in Housing Schemes ;

(B)   an experiment in the technique of Fellowship ;

(C)   new approaches if our Presbyterian witness was to be conserved.

The rebuilding of the actual Conventual Buildings was embarked on partly for its own sake, but more as a symbol of the Church " building itself up again with modern material on an old foundation " and also to provide a common task which would allow " the experiment in the technique of Fellowship " to have a real and not an artificial focus.

It is one thing to outline an experiment, it is another thing to embark on it. But it can be said without false pride or modesty that the first full year's working proved itself to be profoundly worth while.

Teams.

(A)   For years the Church has been committed to experiments in Team work, but a lack of volunteers has made any full experiment hang fire. But after fifteen months of the Community in action we were in a position to offer twelve young ministers to the Church—all of whom were prepared to serve for less than the ordinary assistant commands ; all of whom had had the experience of Iona ; all of whom were free to go to those places that manifestly require a more adequate staffing. In every case they recorded that their experience in Iona in worship, discussion and common life, had fitted them more adequately to serve the Church in its present problems. They are now gone out to needy places.

Fellowship.

(B)   As an experiment in the technique of Fellowship a lot was achieved and much was learnt that could be applied to future years and so improve the experience. The remarkable group of

artisans who offered their services—not one of whom was a misfit—
were the greatest possible assistance in keeping our discussions in
the realm of reality ; in correcting false impressions of the work
that lies before us ; in challenging our complacency by their almost
universal agreement (loyal Churchmen though they were) that the
Church is too much inclined to be a " class show." They were also
of assistance in the genuine contribution that they made to our
worship. Times without numbers they were our leaders in the
actual practice of Christianity in the devastatingly important
realms of unselfishness, forbearance, and reverence. This—perhaps
the most unusual aspect of our experiment, and in some minds
within the Church the least important—proved to be of the greatest
value. I would go so far as to say that, at the present juncture at
least, to leave it out of any future planning would be to end the
essential value of the experiment.

But in the event it was found that the technique of Fellowship
was enriched this summer in further ways as well. A somewhat
lavish inclusion of visitors resulted in considerable gain. Students
from the Presbyterian Churches of England, of Ireland, of America,
of Roumania, of Switzerland, and of Czecho-Slovakia joined our
community for periods varying from a fortnight to months and
made an understanding of their differing problems much more
enduring than their single appearance at a lecture could ever have
done. Again, had the war not intervened it is more than probable
that applications of the same essential principles for which we
stand would have been made in both England and Ulster. Active
preparations were actually in hand to have teams on similar lines
in both these Churches to join us for the full term in 1940. And
the American has crossed the Atlantic voluntarily pledged to find
out what the right counterpart should be in the life of the Protestant
Church there. In addition the inclusion among the lecturers of
well-known figures in the Church of England and Society of Friends
led to a deeper understanding of their positions also. In a day when
world pressures are unparalleled—when Union is in the air—what
more splendid place could there be for the discussion of our real
principles and the submergence of our prejudices than Iona, which
not only has the whole rich heritage of the past brooding around its
stones, but, by the prophetic insight of its present trust deed,
makes the Abbey the only Church in Christendom that every
denomination can call Home.

A more forthright technique of Fellowship man to man is a need
of the age ; a deeper understanding of our common Presbyterian
witness ; and a more intense drawing together of denominations
also. In all these areas Iona proved itself abundantly worth-while.
But it was an artisan who pulled us all up one evening when we were
discussing how quickly Christendom could unite in face of the
perils of atheism and secular tyranny. " These pressures may make
the problem more obvious," he said very quietly, " but it is surely

not they that should actuate us. Isn't it rather the Father's Love that should draw us together into One Family ? "

Worship.

(C) "New approaches if our Presbyterian witness is to be conserved" were the burden of many lectures and the reason for some experiments. It is perhaps this aspect of our experiment that has led to most suspicion of the scheme and it is difficult to see how the suspicion can most fruitfully be dissolved. That there must be new approaches is admitted in almost every manse in Scotland, and little wonder. The format of our worship, generally, in Scotland is the relic of a magnificent puritan tradition. But Puritanism was not a form of worship, but a philosophy of life ; and a puritan outlook on the week-day had its rightful reflection in worship on Sunday. Scotland's restlessness in this regard to-day is that having in fact resiled from a puritan outlook on a week-day, it persists in the hopeless endeavour not altogether to renounce it on Sundays (which, for instance, we still endeavour to call the Sabbath—with all that that implies). This is called loyalty to our fathers, but is in fact a growing affectation. The form of our worship must somehow be made more truly to reflect the real world in which we live. Most ministers agree to this in private and have in fact entirely capitulated to it in the ordering of our Sunday Schools. It is difficult to understand, therefore, their suspicion of all experiments to extend the same principle to our common worship. It may be that "Govan" connotes to them an equally barren alternative of an escape into a hide-bound past that some assume to be the only meaning in the phrase "the Catholic Tradition." Not for well over a decade has Govan in fact stood for such things—if it ever did. Nor is the Iona experiment any other than a determination to discover those forms of worship most likely to lead a congregation into the presence of the Living God. If such determination leads in part to the use of old approaches, it is not because they are old that they are commended but because they are true. If such determination also leads to the re-affirmation of certain specifically Reformed practices (which Scotland has unnecessarily lost) it is not to pay grudging respect to our more immediate tradition but to welcome the re-affirmation as much as older discoveries. It is not for nothing that St. Martin's Cross stands sentinel over the Abbey, "teacher" as he was of St. Columba. Martin's essential thrust was towards simplicity in worship ; the Celt's eternal protest against clogging elaboration. But Martin drew no line between simplicity and beauty and, with Hilary, presented music once again to challenge Rome's most dirgeful monotones. Such thoughts are our pre-occupation.

Whatever be the hesitation of some critics who persist in pre-judging the issue from afar rather than coming, or even writing, to find out, there seemed little hesitation among those who visited the Island and joined in our worship. Their only astonishment was "at the things they had heard said" when they found the actuality. Throughout the summer months it was the rarest thing to have less than a hundred at the daily evening worship. In the last week of August these services re-affirmed a grand tradition from our more immediate past by being a progressive preparation for the Sacrament of Communion. Nearly two hundred every night gathered for such preparation out of a total of some four hundred and fifty people on the Island.

Here, as in the technique of Fellowship, our ultimate path is hardly plotted yet but immeasurably are we encouraged to go on.

In the actual building operations which sealed us together as a Fellowship of Labour, roads were built, a carpenters' shed erected, the whole Refectory carried to the string course, and the masonry of the upper storey of the Chapter House completed. All the wood for its complete restoration is on the site and the slates are as good as there. Some six weeks' work by ten men would make the Chapter House and Library a place of beauty, once again able to hold her head up without shame and speaking in excited whispers to the Abbey Church itself, encouraging her with the rumour that a completed Refectory comes next.

SOME ACCOUNT OF POSSIBILITIES

If "man's extremity be God's opportunity," it is clear that a time of war should call forth from such spiritual ventures as the Iona Community not a battening of the hatches but rather a crowding on of more canvas. There is not a purpose for which it stands the need of whose prosecution is not made more insistent by the probabilities before us. Should the war be shortened all the problems referred to will emerge again with gathered potency; should the war be long the problems with which almost delicately we were dealing will be found to challenge us as stark imperatives. The problem is not whether the Community should continue but into what new channels it should regulate its forces.

Our files now contain the names and addresses of over three thousand people who have asked for information about it—two thousand of whom are paid up Friends. In the three months ending August 31, over a thousand pounds was subscribed through no other appeal than the dissemination of *The Coracle*, and as a result of the Broadcast Appeal to Scotland only (which got cut off in the middle) almost another Thousand was received. The coffers therefore are not empty. If many spiritual adventures find themselves somewhat in the wilderness to-day, it at least reminds us of the Manna that was found there, and which never failed provided always that it was not hoarded. Materially, therefore, we are in a position to advance, in the belief that if our purpose be of God sufficient sustenance will continue to be our portion.

The following decisions are based on the proposition that we are faced with a war of at least twelve months.

I. As regards Iona itself.

(a) Building. The completion of the Chapter House (now financially provided for) will be undertaken as soon as possible in ways that are wholly feasible.

As regards the Refectory—for which some money is in hand—our original purpose to complete the masonry and roof it before the autumn of 1940 seems likely to be held up by the difficulty of obtaining a sufficient supply of wood. There is, however, at present no difficulty about obtaining the freestone from the mainland which is required in considerable quantities for windows, doorways and courses ; nor is there any difficulty about its transport. Since the war began further supplies have been received and landed.

It is therefore intended next summer to complete the masonry of the Refectory and to embark on masonry work (only) on other parts of the ruins. This would mean that the Artisan side of next summer's operation would be almost entirely confined to masons and would allow of concentration on wood construction and interior completion at a happier time.

(b) The summer session. It does not seem likely that probationers—worth their salt—will apply to spend three summer months in Iona in the midst of a world war. There will, however, surely be a demand by placed clergy for a week of Conference and Retreat in a place apart. It is therefore proposed to run twelve consecutive weeks of such Conferences—with some twenty at each conference—from the beginning of June to the end of August. Three Lecturers would be in residence in each separate month, repeating their course four times. One would be an expounder of the Devotional Life, assisting individual souls to find their bearing again ; one would lead discussions on the best witness that congregations can make in the difficult times in which we live ; and a third would lead discussions on what is the essential task of the Church when the war is over. Some of these weeks would no doubt be handed over also to Divinity students, and others to interested laity. I cannot but feel that such a use of the place would be most profitable, in keeping with the essence of our original purpose, and might prove to be of the greatest benefit in revealing to many, who have not yet had the opportunity of discovering, what the Iona Community seeks to stand for in the life of the modern Church.

II. As regards the mainland.

However profitable the use of Iona may prove to be in wartime, as outlined above, the Community was originally conceived to assist the adequate staffing of the Church and to give some experience of Community living both in work and worship. If Iona is presently impracticable for such a centre, is there any way in which this purpose may continue to be fulfilled ? We believe there is—it is to transfer " an experiment in common living " to the mainland during the winter months.

Before outlining the proposal, as I am known to hold certain views about resort to war and as the men most likely to be affected are men who will be of military age, it is essential that I should make some reference to that issue.

If anything that is formed is to continue to be known as the Iona Community it cannot stand for anything essentially different to that for which it was formed. And the Community has always been broad-based as regards applications of the Faith. It has already had within its membership men who were destined for the army both as soldiers and as chaplains, and also pacifists. The Community is neither pacifist nor non-pacifist—which is a reflection of the actual situation in the Church to-day. Anything we form on the mainland must have its doors open to all—as any Church has anyway. But just as our soldier members would be untrue to themselves if they now resigned from the army, I must also record that I feel I would also be untrue to myself if I now renounced the views I hold.

I cannot sum them up here, but whether the war be long or short I am convinced that the next decade will witness amazing changes in the kind of civilisation we have known. The process which every competent critic of sociology has prophesied during recent years is likely to be enormously accelerated. What relation the present hostilities have to the emergence of that new order I do not know. I only know that what God wills will happen and that He can make the wrath of man to praise Him. I resile from any conviction as to how that will happen.

The one supreme conviction that I cannot away from—and without any dramatics—am quite willing to die for is that only the spiritual can mould any future worth having for the world.

Men will have different emphases as to how a spiritual witness is best preserved amidst the horror of war, and it is of paramount importance that we mutually respect our several positions. I am convinced that God is calling some of His followers to stand for positions that are almost bound to be unpopular and that to resile from those convictions would be—for them—consciously to let down even the men who are fighting at the front. My old commander, Douglas Haig, once said that the job of the Church was to be as courageous in spiritual things as he expected soldiers to be in military things. In what were practically the dying words of Lord Allenby we were reminded once again that "the fruits of even victory are dead sea fruits." Somewhere here lies, I believe, a challenge to the Church that it has not fully faced and a depth of witness it has not plumbed. The thought is strongly present with me that unless the Church has this witness somewhere within it, She will have no more to say to the world at the other end of the tunnel than She had to say at the end of the last war. If the Church refuses to allow such a witness within itself then it seems to me we will already have achieved that Totalitarianism—that subservience of the Spirit to the needs of the moment—against which we are supposed to be fighting that it may be banished from the earth.

I have touched on my personal views to make a little more clear something of the atmosphere of the Community in any wartime setting. It is not that it should be pacifist but should be a harbour for the truth that the Church must make room for all applications of the Christian ethic. I visualise a place where soldiers could be as happy to come as pacifists, for its atmosphere would be that freedom of thought for which a battle is on not only at the front but throughout the world—that freedom of thought which alone will get the world out of its ditch.

Its purpose would be to serve the Church in any sphere that opened to it and would be open to both clergy and laity to join. Here one touches on the problem of men of military age. Probationers and students have now been released from the obligation to serve, but whether a man is a pacifist by conviction or has decided that he can do more for his country by following a spiritual profession than by joining up, we seem to be placed in a most onerous position. Willy nilly we are exempted by the Christian legislation of the State ; we are debtors to the system we condemn ; we are safe in our beds by the process of the military. To create a Brotherhood that merely discounts this world's warfare and continues to exist as if nothing had happened seems ultimately to cut across the whole original purpose of the Community, which refused to be cut off and cloistered and embarked on the harder task of being in the world and not of it.

If the doubt is sometimes expressed whether any spiritual lead is likely to come—after the war—from those who, whatever their personal reservations, seem to the common mind to be acquiescing in the inevitable implications of unrestricted warfare, it is equally certain that no spiritual lead will come either from men who wash their hands of the whole pot boiling, spin high-blown theories of their superiority to the madness—and stumble perhaps into the shoes of someone who has gone to the wars, to draw a higher pay ! To say vaguely that we have " a spiritual message to conserve " that justifies our abstention—and do nothing much more than say it vaguely—will neither enlist the best nor tend to creative thought. Thus if the atmosphere is to be one of Freedom we must at least be pledged to serve the State utterly in the most dangerous way we can find in such areas that do not conflict with conscience. Civilian Home Service is no longer merely gathering potatoes or tending cows and there does exist in our towns a potential chance of danger at least equal to that risked by many in the fighting forces on the Home Front. Further, we must take care that those who join it do not find themselves in better paid positions than those who go to the front.

With that preamble we can now outline the plan with at least a chance of it not being totally misunderstood.

I suggest :

1. That a Community be set up attached to a Church in Glasgow or Edinburgh, continuing the name of the Iona Community and expressing its purpose in wartime.

2. That its place of common worship be in the Church, and the Community be housed in an adjacent building.

3. That those who join it should be content with a pay that is comparable with what a soldier gets when allowance has been made for his clothes and upkeep—that in this regard we would be in material things at least not ahead of them in comfort or possessions.

4. That they should offer their services to the Church to be sent in teams of two wherever the Church may need them. Four places are likely to require them :

   (a) Housing schemes ;
   (b) Improvised huts in places where there are large populations, but where the building of Churches is held up ;
   (c) Church of Scotland Army Huts where men are required in charge ;
   (d) Country charges where evacuees create a new problem —not infrequently in the hands of older men who cannot cope with the new dimensions.

5. That their livelihood be guaranteed to them for at least a year.

6. That all who join should spend not less than six weeks at the Community Headquarters, living the common life, studying their probable vocation, helping if time allows in the work of the Parish, and worshipping in Community. This would not only allow them to review the essential truth for which the Community stands, but would mean that in the work to which they go they would know they were being prayed for and would have a home base through which they could exchange notes of problems in their various departments and to which they could return from time to time.

7. An endeavour would also be made to create at Headquarters a panel of "thinkers"—from the University—who would meet regularly with the Community that all might keep constantly before them what the witness of the Church is to be when the war is over. A tragedy of the last war was that at the end the Intellectuals had the answer, but were out of touch with Mainstreet. It is hoped that the constant interaction of Christian Thinkers with a specific centre somewhere in Mainstreet might lead to a post-war Christian Propaganda both informed and in touch with popular opinion.

8. Arrangements would also be made to open the door of the Community to men preparing for the ministry and still at the University who—in some affiliated way—might give their vacations

in the work of soldiers' huts, etc., and enter the Community on a full-time basis when their course was over.

. . . .

It is felt that some such scheme as above outlined would not only be a justified continuation of the Community in terms of the war, but might meet a pressing need that exists among many probationers and students who are at present restless, desiring to serve the Church forthrightly in these tremendous days, but unable to find an avenue in any way comparable to the service that men are willingly rendering to their country. Unless some such scheme finds fulfilment it is feared that some of our best men, both students and probationers, will become impatient of vague references to the urgency of spiritual needs and will fall out of the Army of the Lord at a time when the very best are most urgently required.

. . . .

Finally, the old, old question of finance. It is suggested that the Community should embark on the project on its own finances in the hope that if the scheme became actuality the Church would undertake the payment of the men as they were drafted into position and in the Faith that if this for any reason was delayed money would continue to come in in precisely that measure that was required for the work of the Kingdom. It always does so long as it is the work of the Kingdom. If it proved to be not of the Kingdom then manifestly the sooner it stopped the better.

——o——

REMEMBRANCE.

[To I. A. M.]

With our heart's eyes
We see again
Iona's gleaming
Shell-white shore :
The blue-green tides
Untwist where curled
And glossy sea-wrack
Floats wave-swirled ;
The sunlight glints
Through falling spray ;
The grey mist hides
Ben More.

What happy things
Remembrance sees
Within this world
Of memories !

PUTTING THE CLAPPER ON THE WHIP

THE foregoing article gives sufficient picture of our essential purpose, hedged about by war. This note is to sketch in some of the foreground details. The Rev. R. V. S. Wright, minister of the Canongate Parish, in Edinburgh, who has gone off as a chaplain, has invited us to try out ' the war-time equivalent ' in connection with his Parish, and we have taken over his house —in the very centre of the district—till May, 1940. As his *locum tenens* is Rob Fulton, one of the first of the Iona men, the co-operation should be a joy, and the Presbytery of Edinburgh is being asked to give its blessing to the scheme. The Canongate Parish is one of the most historic in Edinburgh, including in its domain both the Palace of Holyrood house and Arthur's Seat. It also includes some of the most congested closes in Edinburgh—though they are half of what they were but a few years back—and many empty ones await reconditioning. A sizeable enough parish, however, remains, and when the Community tackle its visitation we will have the opportunity of meeting the folk who will one day be moving out to one section of the housing schemes. To grasp the old environment will be a tremendous advantage in facing the new.

The House is ideal. It is one of the old town mansions that used to flank the Royal Mile, set back a space from High Street. It stands opposite the Canongate Church, where daily service is already held, and which will form the place of daily worship for the Community, as for the Parish.

It is known already that some probationers who normally would have come to Iona next summer will come to us instead, earlier in the year, and we hope to institute a similar course of study to that outlined later in the *Coracle*—' Some Summer Memories.'

In place of the work of building, our afternoons will be occupied in Parish visitation, and for our lectures we will be able not only to draw on men in Edinburgh, but make effective contact with actual housing scheme problems.

The course will, however, be somewhat shortened. Two instead of three months will be spent in the Canongate, before men go out in pairs to serve the Church. The middle of March till the middle of May will be our busiest time, when men come down from the Divinity Halls; but prior to that we hope that some probationers will also come.

Not only will men go out to Housing Schemes, but we hope to make a centre and a training place for men who go to Army Hutments. Of how the thing plans out we intend to write in the next number of the magazine. What chiefly fills our minds is gratitude to Ronny Wright for a roof-tree—and to the Session of the Canongate for risking our co-operation.

THE READING OF THE BIBLE

ENCLOSED with this copy of the *Coracle* there has been sent to every 'Friend of Iona Community,' a 'Christmas Card' in the form of a booklet, *Towards Christmas*. No! they are not provided out of the Community funds—that would hardly be a present.

They are, in the first place, a gesture of gratitude for all that the Friends of Iona Community have meant to us in the past summer. In the second place they are the first of the 'Iona Community Publications,' and introduce you to the kind of thing that we hope to publish from time to time as aids to worship and devotion, especially in the housing schemes that are our province, but also, we hope, for general purchase.

A word about this publication. If the Reformed Faith is really to grip the minds of men it is quite certain we must get back— more of us—to the regular reading of God's Word. There has been a terrible falling off in these last decades, due to several causes. Vast numbers still want to read it but somehow . . . well, sometimes it is the print of our Bibles that makes it difficult . . . then again, if we are honest we are not quite sure where to begin again . . . not sure which 'bits' of the Old Testament will enlighten and which merely mystify us. And so a great many of us do not open it as often as 'we are always meaning to do.'

This booklet is simply meant as an aid to start again. There was never a better time for that. The crisis in the world . . . the approach of Christmas . . . the increased opportunities of reading and of quiet that the Black-out affords to many . . . all conspire to turn our thoughts to what God is saying to the world. It is a splendid season to embark on good resolutions, before they become altogether too top-heavy at the New Year!

So we hope you may care to use it—or to pass it on; for, of course, we know that many of our friends are regular readers of the Bible already. But then we also know that they will be the first to agree that it is a good thing to present the Word in ordered sequence and in good print, as we have sought to do here. They may even care to read these passages in addition to their own.

Indeed, the great reason for its circulation with the *Coracle* is to help a little to make the Friends themselves something of a Community—and not just a list of subscribers. We want to feel one with them, not only in our main project, but in our hopes and prayers for the sake of Scotland.

If anyone wants more copies to send to friends, especially those in the Forces, the address of the Hon. Secretary of the Iona Publications can be found at the end of the booklet.

[*Later*—It is an encouragement to know that some 20,000 copies of this booklet have been sold to Parish Ministers in one week!]

PRAYER

THE Iona Community is concerned with the building of an Abbey. It is also concerned with the impact of the Gospel on other structures than stone—the impact of the Gospel on the international structure, on the industrial and the economic structure. We believe ' the whole creation groaneth, waiting for the revealing of the sons of God.' It is also concerned with the ancient gift to the Church of the power to heal. You say it is concerned with a lot of different things ? Precisely, no. All these are one thing—THE IMPACT OF THE GOSPEL ON THE PHYSICAL.

Our real purpose in building the Abbey at all is to make a picture of that. It is where we have gone wrong. So cloistered have men made the Faith—men who pretend to scorn cloisters !— that millions to-day think that Christ ' only has to do with ' the wreckage of individual sinners ! They forget He stilled the storm ; they forget He fed the multitude ; they forget He healed men's bodies ; they forget He is Lord of ALL. He is the Lord of Nature ; the Key to Economics ; the Physician of the whole man.

It was very moving the extent to which folk made use of us last summer when we offered specifically to pray for individuals and for causes. From distant parts of England and from furthest Scotland came requests for prayer—to the place where, in bygone days, great cures were wrought through prayer. At one time over forty specific requests stood upon the Board within the door. More moving still were the answers that came. Gratitude for feverish fears allayed, gratitude for changes that doctors found it hard to account for, and gratitude, in two cases, from men appointed to die but among whose last messages were words of thanks for the comfort that had been theirs in the knowledge that men prayed.

We are very small and backward children in these things. Not tall enough yet even to try to put in the key that will open the door for Christ to enter in and cleanse our economics. Not faithful enough yet for Christ to use us much in healing. He alone can increase our stature. He alone can give us Faith. THE ONE THING WE CAN DO AND MUST DO IS TO PRAY. And take courage in the thought that He likes the prayers of children best.

It is a great joy that the existence of a continuing Community in winter time makes possible this year a similar obedience by the Fellowship in Canongate Parish Church.

Will you send us your requests ?

SOME SUMMER MEMORIES

'WHAT is the point of young ministers kicking their heels in Iona as a preparation for the ministry ? ' Well, there is nothing like asking blunt questions ; and they are all the better of blunt answers—'the preparation for the ministry envisaged by the Iona Community covers NOT merely the three months spent in the Island, but the whole course of two years in the Island and on the mainland. The three months on the Island is a minimum time to come to grips with the kind of problems that are likely to face them and to experiment in that kind of disciplined life without which we are unlikely to face at all the very difficult days that lie ahead of the Church.' Further, our questioner (and the good man exists) can hardly know Iona and certainly cannot have known the programme plotted for our first full summer experiment.

If there is one grave criticism, indeed, that can be levelled at our initial programme it is that it was much too full. It may be of interest to record a typical day.

Morning

It was a practice of the Celtic Clergy to bathe in the sea EVERY DAY OF THE YEAR. (And that, by the way, is very interesting. They had a strong sense of the unity of body with spirit ; physical health was for them an essential mark of Holiness, which is the old English word for healthiness. For them, the body was not ' the enemy of man '—as it almost became for many of ' the religious ' later—but of great moment as the Temple of the Holy Ghost. Interesting, because it is all very modern . . . but it must get an article to itself in some future issue !). It cannot be said that we all rose to the practice of bathing every morning before our day commenced, but it started the day for some. Reveille at 6-45 was rigorous enough. Breakfast at 7-30 was followed by morning worship in the Abbey at 8 o'clock, from which the artisans went out to the building of the walls for the rest of the morning and the ministers went into the daily redding-up of the Community House. A building of thirty-five rooms and passages is problem enough for the inexpert, but daily it was kept in trim by a strictly ordered division of labour. At 9-30 in the Abbey there was a period of half-an-hour of directed prayer and meditation for the ministers, and thereafter we gathered in the common room for the lecture of the day. There are recorded later the men who were good enough to come and spend each a week with us and—in five lectures—tackle their particular subject. From 11 till 12-15 ' to your tents, O Israel ' was the command, and men, each in their own small room, had time to themselves.

Afternoon

After a mid-day meal—a time that is best remembered perhaps by the incursion of dozens of tourists every other day, in their all too hurried tour of Abbey and Community House—the Community as a Fellowship embarked on the manual labour. Till five the ministers were the hewers of wood and drawers of water to the skilled artisans as they erected Carpenters shed or mixed cement ; or they were off to the glebe to tend the vegetables or lift potatoes ; or they were laying the roadway ; or (and perhaps in the memory of some this last should be in block capitals) they were carrying the large boulder stones from the retaining wall to where the masons laid them again, in Refectory course or Chapter gable. There had been difficulty about the best stone for the rebuilding, but it was by permission of the Office of Works that we dismantled the low wall that surrounds the grounds to find the very thing we were looking for, for the good reason that the retaining wall had originally been built out of the ruins of the Abbey. The best result of this has been that the portions rebuilt this summer now contain stones—some of them actual carved doorposts—of precisely the weathering of the ruins themselves. Their transportation by hand-barrow taxed the strength and not infrequently the patience of the labouring clergy, but it was a service without which the building could never have achieved the pace that it did.

And Night.

Tea at five-thirty—again ' ordered,' (as were all the meals), by the ministers—was not the end of the day. Two nights a week we had elaborate choir practice under the strict remonstrance of a minister from Czecho-Slovakia. By the force of his enthusiasm he somehow welded us into a choir that was soon able to carry through the daily services—with some twenty-five items a week—without instrumental accompaniment ; we owe him much. Again, on Mondays the ministers between them visited each of the forty houses on the Island to bid welcome to new visitors and to answer their innumerable questions as to what we were at. This was a going out ' two by two ' that was invariably preceded by a short act of worship and a foretaste of what our purpose was to be in near days to come. And on other evenings there were herdboys to entertain, challenges to be taken up at hockey or at football, or discussions that could not be let alone. The service in the evening at 10 p.m.—where we were always joined by so many from the Island—was the end of a day in which there had been indeed too little time ' to kick our heels.' More time must be found in future years unashamedly to ' stand and stare ' in that most wonderful of islands.

And yet there was some respite. Our theory was the five day week. We kept well at it till tea on Friday, and thereafter, till the worship of Sunday called us, all could follow much their own devices. Some took rods to fish the lochs of Mull ; others took boats to tempt the mackerel and whiting—a few of them (for truth is sacred) experimented once with this, but not again ! and all became conversant with the wonder of the place in walk and picnic. Nor was hockey and football our only contact with the summer crowds. The theory of the thing is not that we be cloistered ; the theory is more demanding and more difficult, it is that resolutely we remain in the world but seek to set a standard that is not ' of it.' And so at concert, dance and gathering—and Friday was the night for them—the community mingled with the life of the place. And if folk questioned that decree the golden opportunity was given us to remind the questioner that the Community of God is not a separate growth from this world's ways, but intertwines it, peculiar, but conjoined, cleansed and cleansing by its discipline in the dust. The New Community—for which the world is waiting—will never grow up ' over against ' ; its emergence will be in and through the present, nurtured by the priesthood of all, born of God.

. . . . .

The Purpose of our Lectures.

Three things demand the Church's quick pre-occupation. The discipline of its clergy ; the mode of our worship ; the environment of modern lives. So we welcomed first of all Dr. G. S. Stewart and Dr. Maxwell. Dr. Stewart came to tell us of the life of personal devotion ; Dr. Maxwell of the principles of worship to which the Christian Faith has always returned to make its corporate witness. I suppose that neither would mind me saying that the first is mostly known as an Evangelical and the latter as a high churchman— however much they both would remonstrate at any such division. It was therefore grand to find the first assuring us of the benefits that come from a constant recollection of the Creed and the use of responses, and the second man protesting that no ' formal ' worship meant anything at all except it be infused at every point by a zeal for the Good News for every single creature. I dare to suggest that if the notes taken of these two sets of lectures—one the evangelical, the other the high church—were shown to a critic, he would be at a loss to say which belonged to which. The glad confusion is of the essence of our purpose !

Of the actual environment of modern charges, and how folk are searching everywhere for Community, Jack Stevenson came to tell us of the country places, and a group of ministers from the housing schemes discussed with us about the towns. George Candlish—prizeman in chemistry, and now a parish minister— assured us, in another week, that the Church had nothing, only superficial scientists anything, to fear from the way in which things were tending in that quantitative world. Then Eric Fenn, H. G. Wood and Roy Whitehorn invaded us from England—why is it that we have to look down south for men on fire with apprehension at the growing chasm that exists between men's worship and their work ? They all had things to say, so vast, so utterly disturbing, that we felt inclined to burrow back into our pleasant, if confined, domains of ' parish visitation.' But they would not let us ; for what they had to say, above all things, we had come. And when we were well nigh lost in the contemplation of man's ingratitude to man, it was a solace to find Dr. Coutts, of Melrose, among us, flourishing a rapier for theology as the only right way through. (The fact that Karl Barth's son had just left us—he had wielded a positive battleaxe—made Coutts's more delicate thrusts and parries even more enthralling).

In the closing week, that almost synchronised with war, Tubby Clayton came among us. His declared subject was ' Hounds of Heaven, Ancient and Modern,' and turned out to have nothing to do with that almost nationally famous black spaniel that invariably accompanies him. Nor, truth to tell, had the title much to do with what he said to us. But there are bigger things to be learnt than consistency, and he gave us what we needed most if we were to go as issionaries indeed. He gave us a glimpse of his own rich love of men, just for their own sake and for God's sake, for the sake of Jesus Christ our Lord. And may God forgive us for our lack of it, many of us in the ministry of His Church in Scotland.

G. F. M.

THE WORK IN THE HOUSING SCHEMES
THE GIFT FOR TEAM WORK.

A S WAS outlined in the last *Coracle*, the normal intention would have been to engage in five missions in five different Housing Schemes to which it was intended our men should go. Nor were they to be ' just a babel of confused sounds ' as missions can sometimes be, if they are not duly prepared for. The central principle of the Iona Experiment is that it is ' the Community of the Redeemed ' that God has chosen as his agent for Redemption. His Church is the instrument He has ordained to witness to His Gospel and to gather His own. What had been plotted, therefore, was that in each district there should be a week in autumn when THE CONGREGATION should be recalled to the meaning of its heritage ; that it is not primarily there to be ministered unto by its minister, but that the Fellowship of Christ in any district are placed there of God to be ' fellow labourers ' WITH the minister in winning back the alien ' world ' that surrounds them. This autumn week would have been followed up by intensive visitation —by the congregation—in the area in preparation for the SECOND week in spring, when a week's mission would have been conducted among all who cared to come. It had been Dr. MacLeod's intention to spend ten weeks of the winter months in conducting these dual presentations of the Faith in the five districts.

The Black-Out threw out the possibilities of a really full experiment being made, the evacuation further complicating the immediate needs in most of the districts that had been chosen. But the purpose stands, and we are in high hopes that in at least two of the districts the full programme may yet be carried out, with a somewhat changed programme to meet changed needs. We believe that as a result of these experiments we will be in a position to carry out the full original programme even though the war should continue.

It is for this kind of experiment that teams are so necessary. For all the ceaseless propaganda of the Home Board, few folk yet realise the immensity of the challenge that faces the Church. Over a million people since 1920 have moved into areas where churches have had to be built. Over thirty churches or halls have been put up, but even that fine record hardly meets the case. Men are attempting to work parishes of anything between 12,000 people and 20,000 alone or with the sole assistance of a Church Sister. Inevitably, unless something is done in these areas THE MAJORITY OF THE PEOPLE will lose touch with the Church ; the Church will cease to be a national institution and will become the interest of a sect. Scotland's essential relationship to the Faith will become a thing of the past.

Many of our towns with a population of 20,000 have eight or nine places of worship ; it is a scandal that ' new towns ' with a similar population should be left to break the heart of a single ministry. So, to these places Iona wants to send its men.

AN ENCOURAGING GIFT.

It was therefore a great encouragement to the Home Board— when the war further intensified the problem by preventing the building of more churches—to have the offer made to provide ' four teams of two ' for four needy places for the next six years. And it was a great encouragement to the Iona experiment. For, while it is not a condition that only men from Iona must form these teams, the condition is that the experiments in these places ' would take account of the kind of training there provided for as a good basis for this approach to the problem.'

Iona men are, in fact, being appointed to the primary experiments, and there lies before us, without a peradventure, the chance to prove our mettle along the lines foreshadowed in the commencement of this article.

We hope in the next number of the *Coracle* to tell you some particulars of the places where they go, and some details of our plans of campaign.

THE IRON BELL IN THE SEAWEED

[*This Extract from the land settlement book of Iceland—an account of an Iona man in the eighth century—is an encouragement to all who embark on Missionary endeavours.*]

"AUR-LYG was the name of a son of Hrapp, the son of Beorn Buna. He was in fosterage with Bishop Patrec, the Saint in the Southreys (Hebrides). A yearning came upon him to go to Iceland, and prayed Bishop Patrec that he would give him an outfit. The Bishop gave him timber for a church and asked him to take it with him, and a plenarium, and an iron church bell, and a gold penny, and consecrated earth to lay under the corner-posts instead of hallowing the church, and prelates to dedicate the church to Colum-cella.

Then spake Bishop Patrec:—"Wheresoever thou turnest in to land, dwell only there where three fells can be seen from the sea and a firth running between each fell, and a dale in each fell. Thou shalt sail to the furthest (southernmost); there shall be a shaw there, and further south under the fell thou shalt light on a clearing and three stones raised or set up there. Do thou raise thy church and homestead there."

Aur-lyg put to sea, and in a second ship with him a man named Coll, his sworn brother. They kept company out. On board Aur-lyg's ship was a man whose name was Thor-beorn Sparrow; another called Thor-beorn Talcni; the third, Thor-beorn Scuma. They were the sons of Bead-were Bladderpate. But when they they came where they might look out for the land, there arose a great storm against them, and drove them west, about Iceland. Then Aur-lyg called upon Bishop Patrec, his foster father, to bring them ashore, and vowed that he would give the place a name after his name, wherever he should first come ashore. And after that they were but a little while ere they got to land; and he brought his ship in to Aur-lyg's haven, and called the firth Patrec's Firth, therefore. But as for Coll, he called upon Thor, or Thunder. They were parted in the storm and he reached the place called Colls-wick and there his ship was wrecked. His crew got to land, some of them, and shall be told after. And in the spring Aur-lyg fitted out his ship, and sailed away with all that he had; and when he came south, off Faxes-mouth, he saw the fells that had been spoken of to him, and he knew them. And then the iron bell fell overboard and sunk in the sea. But they sailed in along the firth, and went in to the land at the place that is now called Sand-wick on Keelness, and there lay the iron bell in the seaweed.

Aur-lyg took up his abode at Esia-rock (Clay-rock), by the rede of Helge Beolan, his kinsman, and took land in settlement between Mogils-river and Oswif's becks. He built a church at Esia-rock as was commanded him."

SERMON BROADCAST FROM IONA ABBEY

TO THE BRITISH EMPIRE ON (WHAT TRANSPIRED AS)
THE LAST SUNDAY BEFORE WAR WAS DECLARED

Mark xvi. 15.—*Jesus said unto them, Go ye into all the world and preach the Gospel to the whole creation.*

AFTER the close of this service the Week's Good Cause—on the Scottish wave length only—is The Iona Community; this new experiment of our Church Reformed.

It is a company half-craftsmen and half-clergy, pledged to re-assert our presbyterian witness; to live and work and pray together in the building of this Abbey, whence, please God, some twenty different clergy will go out each year to serve the Church forthrightly wherever the need for them is urgent.

Towards the ending of last week (as newspaper headings grew larger and possibilities more ominous) a candid friend upon the road asked me the direct question—" What's your subject? The national purpose of your small community or the vast agonising issue that confronts our land and race?" In reply, I almost found myself saying "For all the vast disparity, aren't they in essence just two sides of the same round coin—the relation of Iona to a world confusion?"

I wonder if to-night I can convey to you why I said that?

The New Community found itself on Iona, one might almost say, because of three things—a Stone; a Structure and a Sound; all of them familiar to those who know this island.

I want to speak of them—that stone, that structure and that sound. And to ask you at the end whether this dream of ours to build an Abbey is just an Island Song—remote, pedantic—*or*, under God, in tune with what a dying world most needs.

The first thing that brought us here was a Stone. A stone in the shape of a Cross—St. Martin's Cross, how well you know it, that stands guardian over the entrance to this Church. As if St. Martin said, "You must come to terms with what I thought of Christ if you would enter this Church to-day."

Martin, the Celt; the spiritual father of St. Ninian; the begetter of Columba's every purpose; your creditor and mine in the Faith we hold.

When did he live? Oh, some sixteen hundred years ago; yes, I know what some of you are saying—" What in thunder can he have had to do with the days in which we live? A shadowy monk, I suppose, singing doleful psalms with a company of doleful priests and mumbling doubtful miracles through pagan Scotland!" But no; you're wrong. Martin was an officer in the Imperial Guard of Rome, when that great Empire was still resplendent with the grandest civilization man had ever seen. But Martin knew that the grandeur that was Rome's had had its day; civilised man had overstepped his pride; Nemesis was on him. Even the Church itself was faded with a vestment pride. The thing had become bourgeois; cumbersome; divorced. It was not in touch with men, it missed their common life.

To him once more the immemorial summons came—Go out and preach the Gospel to the whole creation. And so he took commission with the King of Kings. What were his marching orders? Well, if that decaying world was to be saved, Christ alone could save it. But if men were to be found of Christ again, His Church must become simple once more, forthright, missionary; not concerned with the outward, but with the inward. Beauty must come back and freshness; to serve the King of Kings. New ways must be found.

And so he sent his followers out—no, not companies of doleful priests singing doleful songs, but groups of twelve—among whom only two were priests. The rest were agriculturists and craftsmen, doctors and teachers—" Because," he said, " the *common ways* must be won again for God; not just the spiritual segments of men's lives." And by that grand insistence Martin restored a Faith to Scotland.

Was he so old-fashioned after all? Civilization doomed ... man had overstepped his pride ... Nemesis was on him ... are all these just phrases from the books about the decline and fall of Rome? Aren't they all about us once again, in the very air we breathe? The Church must become missionary again, simple, forthright. New ways must be found—that was Martin's thrust.

Well, that stone brought us here; the challenge of that man for modern days. In modern terms—" Martin's reading " of the Cross.

The Second thing that brought us here was a Structure.

A ruined one. This Abbey, where to-night you pray with us in spirit, is not a ruin. (it used to be; they built it up again, most beautifully, some thirty years ago.) But just beside it, here where my hand is pointing there is ruin still. It is the part where men once lived the common life to serve the Abbey Church—the old conventual buildings. Its roof, high heaven; its walls moss-covered. We've come to roof it again that men may learn to live and pray in unison; and find fellowship within its walls.

Yes! I think I know what you are saying—" Ah, but those days are past; they served their generation; it's the modern world we're living in and the thing is half-dead; whatever else will save it, it's no good looking back." Is that what you are saying? But hold a minute. What is the real sickness of this modern world ? Is it the absence of the Church ? I assure you, no ! The Church was never more efficient than in the days in which we live. Services galore, Churches clean and tidy.

BUT, BUT the thing most happens on a Sunday. It is the week-day life of men that lies in ruins. The economic structure—the industrial, the international—these are the grave concerns bereft to-day of Spirit. These are the places where men have to live and move and have their being—and the roof of them is falling in !

And oh, how we Churchmen burrow—you and I—to keep our eyes from seeing. Oh, the dugout we have made of Sunday, not because we are blind, but because we dare not raise our eyes to see the ruin of our " every day "—which is what *Jesus* came to build !

And so we dabble with the non-essentials. New tunes for hymns become our passion—lest we hear the vast disharmony in the soul of modern man. Great organs with a hundred stops must play their loudest diapasons lest we hear those whirring wheels, at a thousand revolutions, that deafen engineers.

Every mortal circumstance in the broken world around us is positively shouting that we seek again the open air and risk the falling debris.

There is not a man who is sane to-day who does not know that only the spiritual can save the world. The real sickness is that the spiritual has become divorced from the common life of men and got boxed up in the Sunday. Our Fellowship is dandified, anaemic, periodic ; while men are dying everywhere for the lack of friends.

We must put again " God's Rooftree " over the Community Life of men—over what they do on week-days.

And so the second thing that brought us here was that ruined structure where men once lived that it might remind us of the ruins of our " everyday."

Men think to-day that God is only interested in the souls of men—which somehow come to flower on Sundays. Men don't believe that God alone can deal with structures too. And so we build this place anew to remind us that God can deal with *stones* ; that He can build up stony structures—as well as bind up stony hearts—if only we will give them back to Him.

We must preach the Gospel again, not just to every creature, but to the whole creation !

And when you come to visit us in four years' time we will show you our library. All the living books of " How to win a modern world for God," which we will study as we live together on the week-days too, before coming back amongst you on the mainland, each winter, with a mission of new ways.

The Last Thing that brought us here was a Sound.

Those of you who know this Island know how its eastern shore lies sheltered, looking out across a narrow strip of water towards the Ross of Mull. But the western shore lies open to the full Atlantic gale.

Sometimes on that eastern sheltered shore you can look out on a sunlit sea as calm as Galilee—but even as you look you hear a strange dull roar. It means a western wind is beating and a heavy sea is thundering on the other shore a mile away. The thing is a parable. What sunlight has glinted (on a larger isle than Iona) in these last years ; what calm, to all appearing has played at the foot of Britain. Yet who dare say that the thundering (that to-night we can hear on distant shores) has not been growing and growing for all who cared to listen ?

But we have not listened, we have played. Well, the game is over, we must listen now.

What are we to do then ? God grant we turn our faces to the that every one must do is to be loyal to the highest that they know. But perhaps—of mercy—the giant wave will merge miraculous once more in what still must be an ugly sea ; we *may* be saved the deluge. That would be miracle enough, but the sea will still be ugly.

What are we to do then ? God grant at least that none of us return to our sand castles. God grant we turn our faces to the breeze at last and go over to look more steadfastly at this storm.

Don't be mistaken ; don't be heretic ; don't be blasphemous ; don't think our present turmoil is beyond the hand of God. This sacred Isle of Iona belongs to God, but the sea is also His. The sunlight on our sheltered coves comes straight from God, but He also rides the storm.

This land of ours, this Britain with all its precious heritage is the gift and creation of our God. But let us resist, like sin, the ghastly modern heresy that a world confusion denotes a God who has lost control.

Don't ask why " God doesn't speak ? " Don't stand amazed at his apparent deafness. Don't half listen for His voice somewhere beyond the storm. IT IS THE STORM THAT IS HIS VOICE. It is the storm that is the voice of the God and Father of our Lord Jesus Christ. It is a storm in the common life of men because the common life of men has been denied to God. Go resolutely toward it, to seek what manner of man is this whom even the wind and waves obey. Care not whether this community be a stable thing or a bubble reputation ; but pray for the one thing left that is worth praying for ; pray to God, with a new found zeal, that men may arise once more—and that right speedily—to preach the old full Gospel to the whole creation.

HOW YOU CAN HELP

By becoming a "Friend of Iona Community."

The minimum subscription is five shillings a year which goes to the rebuilding fund and to the work of the Community. It also entitles you to receive this quarterly during the year.

It is computed that the Restoration and Rehabilitation of the Abbey will cost some £30,000. The Community is further responsible for all its commitments. The Church of Scotland, while blessing the scheme, makes no grants towards its work (other than the teamwork gift notified in this issue).

It is your venture or it fades.

By securing more Friends,

In the May issue of *The Coracle* we asked that the thousand Friends should double their number by May 1940. We apologise for Faithlessness. There were over two thousand Friends by October 1939 ! But that must be doubled again if we are to spread interest in our increasing purpose. A large number of lectures—which always secure more Friends—have been cancelled this year by the Black Out. May we ask Friends to pass on their copy of *The Coracle* to likely folk—to pass on news of our FULL purpose to those with whom they come in contact ? We are delighted to send copies of the magazine for distribution. And we are most grateful to many who have already widened the circle for us.

All communications should be addressed to :
Rev. George MacLeod at either of the addresses referred to
on the front of this magazine.

By Yours Prayers.

For the work of the Community ; for its members working in housing scheme or congested areas ; for its artisans in spreading the message in the places where they work ; and for

THE REVIVAL OF THE FAITH IN SCOTLAND

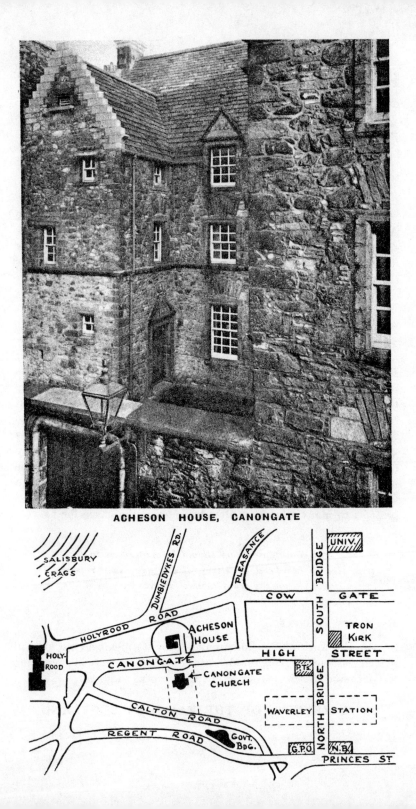

ACHESON HOUSE, CANONGATE

CURRENT PUBLICATIONS OF THE IONA COMMUNITY